| | |
|---|---|
| 13 | OREGON TRAIL |
| 14 | NATIONAL PARKS GULF HIGHWAY |
| 15 | PACIFIC HIGHWAY |
| 16 | ARROWHEAD TRAIL |
| 17 | OCEAN TO OCEAN HIGHWAY |
| 18 | OLD SPANISH TRAIL |
| 19 | KING OF TRAILS |
| 20 | JEFFERSON HIGHWAY |

ARKS TRANS HIGHWAY  18  OLD SPANISH TRAIL

GHWAY

NOTE: NATIONAL OLD TRAILS ROAD SHOWN AS NUMBER 3 PERMANENTLY SIGN POSTED FROM LOS ANGELES TO KANSAS CITY BY AUTO CLUB SO. CAL. LINCOLN HIGHWAY SHOWN AS NUMBER 4 PERMANENTLY SIGN POSTED FROM OMAHA TO ELY BY AUTO CLUB OF SOUTHERN CALIFORNIA. MIDLAND TRAIL SHOWN AS NUMBER 12 PERMANENTLY SIGN POSTED BY AUTO CLUB OF SO. CAL. FROM ELY TO LOS ANGELES.

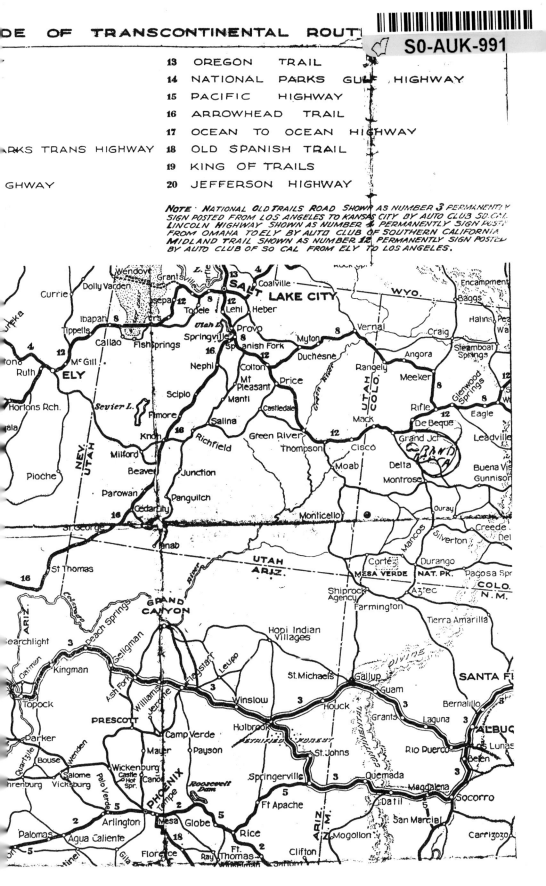

# A MID – CALIFORNIA
# ILLUSTRATED HISTORY

George Emanuels

Other books by George Emanuels

YGNACIO VALLEY 1834-1970

WALNUT CREEK – ARROYO DE LAS NUECES

JOHN MUIR INVENTOR

CALIFORNIA'S CONTRA COSTA COUNTY – AN
ILLUSTRATED HISTORY

OUR FIRST ONE HUNDRED YEARS

CALIFORNIA INDIANS – AN ILLUSTRATED GUIDE

# A MID - CALIFORNIA
# ILLUSTRATED HISTORY

By

George Emanuels

Walnut Creek, California, 1995

ISBN 0-9607520-6-4


Published and distributed by
George Emanuels dba DIABLO BOOKS
1700 Tice Valley Blvd. #150
Walnut Creek, California 94595
Telephone (510) 939-8644 (voice); (510) 943-1358 (fax)

and by
Kings River Press
313 E. Deodar Lane
Lemoore, California 93245
Telephone (209) 924-1766

# Contents

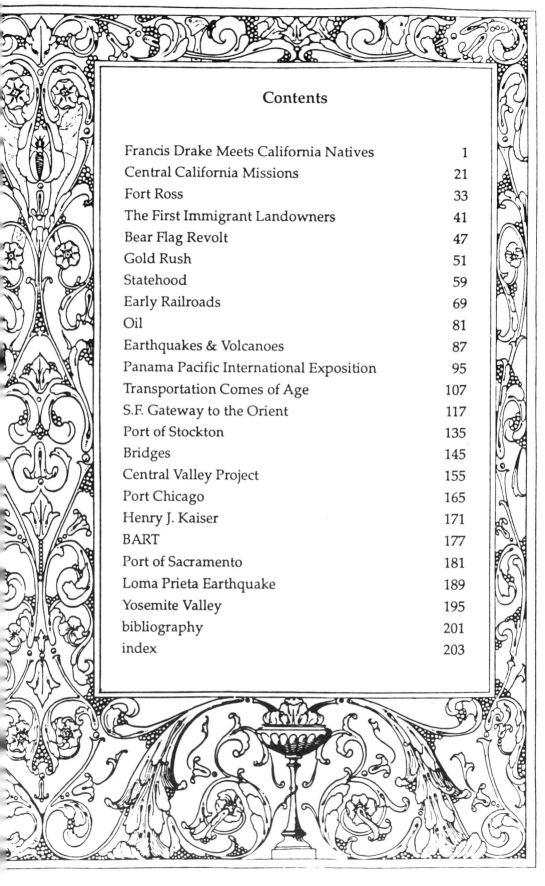

# Acknowledgments

While I am listed as the Author of this book, it came into being as a family affair.

My wife Helen, saw each page first and offered suggestions for their improvement. Son Roger, edited and later typeset the entire work. Son Fred with his wife Claire, corrected my punctuations and proofread too. Our daughter, Joan Pickering, proofread and made a number of suggestions which I acted on to improve and make the book more readable. Fred took several pictures, driving scores of miles in the process.

Many others helped by supplying photographs to whom I will try to give recognition. If I omit anyone I plead for forgiveness. They are: Bob Colin, Janet Joseph, Laura Clark and Robert Halligan of CalTrans. Alison Moncriess, Alan Beilharz, and Toshiro Koruma of the California State Parks have been very helpful. Mary Ellen Baldwin of Davis went out of her way to get me some dates. Clarence Compton, Ned Dodds, William De Poy, Dave Do-play, Bill and Tillie Larkins, Rick Lester, Timothy Moore, William Marshall, William Sturm, Lisa Dapprich, Lynelle Johnson, Patricia Huff, and Robert Watson, thanks to each of you who gave of your special talents.

George Emanuels

# Introduction

On one of my calls on Larry's Book Nook of Walnut Creek, the proprietor, Larry Sydes, ordered some books and then surprised me with, "You know the next book you write is one that I get requests for regularly and don't have."

Larry explained, "People who are leaving the State or going back east for one reason or another, often come in asking for a history which covers our area as well as the country on the way to the mountains through Stockton and Sacramento. They include the area up to Fort Ross on the coast and down to Big Sur. My answer has to be, 'We don't have a book like that.'"

So here is a title which will shed light on what went on here over the last 150 years.

Over that span of time, and not so long ago at that, people have given up riding around our northern counties by horseback, or in a buggy or by stagecoach over rough, unpaved rutted roads. Now we have smooth paved comfortable highways and take them for granted as if they were always here. One hundred years ago riverboats and ferries served the needs of many travelers before highways did.

How did the early Californians turn this Mexican colony into one of the states of the United States? Is it any surprise to learn that the steamships which brought the gold seekers to San Francisco from Panama were powered by two paddle wheels, one on either side? Where in this State was the first scheduled railroad established?

Who were the first immigrants to take up thousands of acres each, gifts of the Mexican Government?

Where did petroleum refining, now so important a part of our economy, commence in our area?

Since electric lights were unknown to the early auto manufacturers, what kind of night illumination did the early cars have?

Why was the Carquinez Bridge so important to our travelers?

Who was the one with the first idea to build the Golden Gate Bridge and the San Francisco-Oakland Bay Bridge? When did each open for traffic? Did trains ever cross the Bay on the Bay Bridge?

These are only a very few questions which are answered in "A Mid California Illustrated History."

Chapters include Earthquakes and Volcanoes, the Panama Pacific International Exposition, the Ports of Sacramento and Stockton, the Central Valley Project and a dozen or more subjects. One covers Francisco Drake Meets California Natives (in 1579) and another the 1989 Loma Prieta Earthquake. All are in pictures as well as words.

George Emanuels

QUEEN ELIZABETH CONFERRED KNIGHTHOOD ON
FRANCIS DRAKE SOON AFTER HE COMPLETED
HIS CIRCUMNAVIGATION OF THE WORLD IN 1580

(World Publishing Co.)

# Francis Drake Meets California Natives

Francis Drake, the first explorer to touch California, landed at the bay which is now named for him. He lived there for thirty-six days in June and July of 1579. The report he made to Queen Elizabeth of England included the helpful treatment he received from the Indians on the Point Reyes Peninsula. He said they brought him a very generous supply of venison and a gruel which resembled mush made from wild grass seeds.

For thousands of years these first Californians had lived in peace, for the best part. They seldom warred on each other, did not despoil the earth or do anything to endanger the environment.

The first explorer unloaded his vessel, the *Golden Hinde*, beached it so that his men might scrape off the barnacles and other sea growth, and made many necessary repairs to the vessel. They refloated the ship, reloaded it, filled their fresh water casks, and stowed the firewood the Indians had brought to the

*(continues on page 5)*

From Arnoldus Montanus, *Die unbekante neue Welt*; the Dapper issue, Amsterdam, 1673

The first European to land in California was Juan Rodriguez Cabrillo who went ashore in Southern California in 1542. The earliest European to visit Northern California was Francis Drake who landed on the Marin County coast of California in June, 1579.

All accounts which survived his voyage emphasize that the Coast Miwok Indians received the commander as they would a deity. Throughout his five-week stay the natives remained both peaceful and friendly.

At the time of his departure the accounts agree, there was much weeping, after seeing their wishes for the Englishmen to remain had failed the Indians.

*In 1599, twenty years after Francis Drake visited the Pt. Reyes Peninsula, Theodor de Bry produced this engraving depicting the welcome the Coast Miwok Indians gave the explorer. While much is fanciful, including the two ships, the* Golden Hinde *came alone. The quiver is genuine. The chief in a headdress and with a deer-skin loin cloth are what we might expect him to be wearing. The nakedness of most of the natives is certainly correctly depicted. The weeping woman at the right apparently fears for the safety of her family as they cower around the fire in spite of the momentous scene going on around them. The conical slab huts were undoubtedly used in a place as fog-bound as Drake's Bay. The Indians undoubtedly rushed over the hills to see a sailing ship and men from another world for the first time. The two closest major villages were one at Olema and a larger one at Nicasio.*

Since Drake completed his voyage more than three hundred years ago, two questions remain unanswered by historians.

How could the two engravers, the one who did the 1673 picture and Theodor de Bry, whose work appeared in 1599, have learned of the details they so accurately rendered? One appeared only twenty years after the event and the other ninety-four years after. De Bry's rendition is particularly accurate in light of what we know from Alfred Kroeber's and Robert Heizer's research in this century about the Coast Miwok.

The second question is how did the explorer find his way to the only channel by which he could sail his ship, the Golden Hinde, from the Pacific Ocean to the Indian Ocean?

One has only to open a map of the Philippine Archipelago to see how difficult a task he faced. Even if he had a chart of the area, though none was available in his century, the instruments he relied on couldn't have answered his needs.

Although the Dutch navigators found their way to Japan in Drake's time, they also had contact with the Portuguese who had sailed into the South China Sea. But the question remains. How could Drake have come by the course which he would need to follow, starting from the north coast of western America, and sail with the unsophisticated instruments more than 4,000 miles, and reach the perfect spot to sail into the Indian Ocean?

shore. With many natives weeping at the signs of their departure, Drake and his crew sailed west and reached England. Drake thus became the first explorer to circumnavigate the globe.

Drake's written report was lost, but what has survived 400 years is the journal of his chaplain published as "The World Encompassed by Sir Francis Drake, Carefully collected out of the notes of Master Francis Fletcher, Preacher, in this imployment, and diverse others his followers in the same. 1628."

"The men for the most part go naked, the women take a kind of bulrushes, and kembing (combing?) it after the manner of hemp make themselves a loose garment, which being knitte around their middles, hangs downe about their hippes, affords them a covering, having also about their shoulders, a skinne of Deere, with the hair upon it.

"Their houses are digged round within the earth and have from the outermost brimmes of the circles clefts of wood set up, and joyned close together at the top like our spires on the steeple of a church; which being covered with earth, suffer no water to enter and are very warm; the door in most part of them performs the office also of a chimney to let out the smoke.

"The King had on his head a cawle of knit-work, wrought upon somewhat like a crownees; ...his guards also having cawles likewise stuck with feathers, or crowned over with a certain downe, which groweth up in the country an herb much like our letuce, which exceeds any other downe in fineness, and being laid upon their cawles, can be no wind be removed.

"Their baskets were made in a fashion like a deep boale, and though the matters were rushes, or such other kind of stuffe, yet was it so cunningly handled, that the most part of them would hold water; about the brimmes they were hanged with peeces of shels of pearles (Broken bits of abalone shells?) and in some places with two or three linkes at a place; and besides this, they

Louis Choris, 1816

*Choris identifies the women on the left and the center as from a Coast Miwok tribelet in Marin County, the one second from the left a Utschuin, an Alameda County tribelet, and the two on the right as Saklans, a Miwok family group in the Walnut Creek area. Over 160 Saklan were baptized at Mission Dolores between 1794-1810. The artist left us this observation of the natives: "I have never seen one laugh. I have never seen one look one in the face. They look as though they were interested in nothing."*

were wrought upon with matted downe with red feathers."

Francis Drake left England on December 15,1577 and reached the Marin County coast in mid-June 1579. After 36 days he departed for England. His total elapsed time for the "World Encompassed" was two years, 10 months, "and some few odde daies beside."

Lowie Museum, Berkeley, Calif.
*These three coast Miwok are on their way to a day of gathering wild seeds. Note the wide mouth baskets in the stern of their balsa. The Marin shoreline is in the background.*

To begin to understand the native Californians, one has only to read Don Gaspar Portolá's account of meeting them. No other explorer came overland before Portolá so his record gives a very true picture of the California Indians before their contact with Europeans.

*Otto von Kotzebue, Russian naval officer and explorer, commanded two voyages around the world. On his first, 1815-17, the artist Louis Choris viewed Central Californian Indians while in port at Monterey. His renditions came to public attention when his book* Pictoresque Autour de Monde *was issued in 1822. This is his impression of Mission Dolores Indians in their ceremonial headdresses.*

Following is the translation of what he saw and experienced along the Indian trail north from San Diego. He set out from his base camp at San Diego Bay on July 14, 1769

"From San Diego — 26 leagues. The Indians of a village…came over unarmed, with unmatched friendliness and peacefulness, made us a present of their poor seeds and were treated by us.

"From San Diego — 33 leagues. A populous village of Indians who received us with great friendliness. Fifty-two of their number came over to our camp, and their chief or headman told us with much pleading...that we should stay and live with them, (that) they would provide us our sustenance.

"From San Diego — 48 leagues. We found a village of heathens, very friendly; at once they visited our quarters with bowls of seed foods, nuts and acorns.

"From San Diego — 58 leagues. A crowd of Indians came over to the camp with a present of seeds, acorns and canegrass honeycomb, a very friendly affectionate folk.

"From San Diego — 64 leagues. Seven chiefs came over with a bountiful present of seeds, acorns, nuts, and pine nuts which they spread before us.

"From San Diego — 73 leagues. We placed our camp next to a temporary village of Indian fishermen who made us a present of more fish than we could eat."

As he continued on, Portolá experienced similar help along the way until his men halted at the barrier in their path, the Golden Gate. Then and only then, did natives show him any hostility.

Without an armed conflict the expedition turned about and headed back to San Diego. From approximately San Luis Obispo south his record states, "The Indians of this town presented us with quantities of fresh and dried fish, a great deal of sardines and bonitos, so that we began, thank God, to see plenty prevail in our camp."

Five years later Fray Pedro Font, the spiritual leader of Anza's California Colony, came north in Portolá's footsteps. While in the Santa Barbara area Font observes, "Yet I saw very few women close at hand, for as soon as they saw us they all hastily hid in their huts, especially the girls, the men remaining outside blocking the doors and taking care that nobody should go inside."

H. R. Schoolcraft, *Indian Tribes of the United States*, 1865

*In the manner traditional among the California Indians who gathered grass seeds, these women are beating the heads of the grass directly into their bearing basket. Note the shapes of the two beaters.*

*Wailaki girls were usually tattooed between the ages 15-17. Though they could be betrothed before puberty most often the promise to marry meant no more than that—it could easily be broken. Brides were purchased and the price was negotiable. At birthing the Wailaki cut the naval cord using a flint blade. Members of this tribe avoided marriage with kin, a practice not often adhered to by neighboring groups.*

Thus the Europeans betrayed the goodwill shown them. Nevertheless, for at least the next fifty years, the natives both north and south, upon meeting the white man for the first time, extended the hand of friendship.

Two hundred years after Drake, the commander of the first ship to sail through the Golden Gate, Frigate-Lieutenant Don Juan de Ayala, wrote of his experience with the natives, "…right from the first day's dealings with the Indians…it was obvious at once how friendly they were. We explained to them by sign that we would be able to eat and sleep there. They (the Indians) had already prepared for them (the shore party) a present of pinole bread made of seeds, and tamales of the same."

For obvious reasons no count of the natives was ever made, but estimates have been made that as many as 360,000 natives lived in California in the very early 1800s. By 1900 probably no more than 15,000 Indians remained.

Many Indians from San Diego to Sonoma and from the coast up into the gold region were made slaves. Every large land-owner but John Bidwell, who came to Butte County in 1841, had his slave quarters. Slaves kept away from their women don't father children, hence the birth rate dropped sharply after the arrival of the Europeans.

Even small ranchers had their captives. One Granville Swift, an illiterate miner, made a fortune by making his natives bring him the results of their digging. When they brought him less than he wanted, he whipped them and confined them at night. He built his stone house, Temelec Hall, in Sonoma in 1858, and again used Indian slaves as workers. When he worked them by day he chained their ankles to cannon balls, and at night chained them to the walls of their barracks.

Indians succumbed to smallpox in large numbers. Epidemics broke out all over California. In 1838, one surfaced to the north of San Francisco Bay within the confines of General Vallejo's jurisdiction, where deaths among the natives were es-

*This view of the San Francisco Presidio and the area in front of it, now Crissy Field, is the work of artist Tilenau who saw this scene in 1806 from the deck of the Russian Ship Juno. This foreign vessel came to S. F. Bay in search of a source of food for the famished Russian colonists in the north. Nikolai Rezenov made arrangements to conduct future trade with the Californians. Six years later when the Russians founded Fort Ross they found the Spanish had changed their minds. They feared the occupation and let the invaders know they wanted no intercourse with them.*

*There had to be a considerable amount of balsa traffic on San Francisco Bay. Early accounts, before 1785, state about 100 persons lived in a village at the mouth of Wildcat Canyon in the East Bay and there were two more on the same shore, one near Rodeo and the other near Pinole, each with between 400 and 500 people. Another indication of a large number of Indians living on the Bay front is the immense shell mound left at Emeryville.*

timated at 60,000 to 75,000. Earlier, in 1828-29, a smallpox epidemic ravaged the mission Indians all through the 21 missions.

Any estimate of those natives who died from gunshot wounds would have to be placed at least at 100,000. Mexican soldiers ambushed them, and when the State joined the Union, the United States Army continued the slaughter. On one foray alone in Sonoma County, Salvador Vallejo, brother of the General, led his Mexican troops and his Indian allies, the Suisuns, north pursuing the Sotoyomi tribe. A Sotoyomi had stolen one

Louis Choris, 1816

*These Indians at Mission Dolores might gamble all day and night losing down to their last piece of clothing which the loser would hand over to the winner, leaving the game naked, yet he would show no concern and go about his day's duties as if he had won. Natives often gambled away their store of acorns or dried fish leaving their families without a winter's sustenance.*

From Alexander Forbes, *A History of Lower & Upper California*, 1877
*This is the interior of a central California sweathouse or* temescal, *undoubtedly earth covered, as seen by Forbes.*

of the general's mules. The tribe seized Vallejo's envoy who had been sent to return the animal and tortured the man. In revenge, the expedition killed 800 Indians and took 300 more prisoner. Certainly the prisoners became Vallejo's slaves.

When settlers moved into Mendocino, Humboldt and Del Norte Counties in the 1850s, they began destroying some of the Indians' way of life. The U.S. Army went in to keep peace between the natives and the whites, which resulted in more Indian bloodletting. Indians took revenge on the settlers and the settlers did the same on the natives. Every Indian became fair

Louis Choris

*Louis Choris watched the Mission Indians dance what originally were their native rites in front of Mission Dolores near Yerba Buena, where they were allowed to perform them by the padres because it brought joy into their otherwise dull, routine lives.*

*The Indians were forced to listen to masses in a language they didn't understand and given punishment if they failed to observe the Catholic rites. When not in the chapel they all had jobs given them, the least constructive work, often repetitive and therefore dull.*

*Instead of the soldiers doing the hard work needed at the Presidio the Mission priests loaned the neophytes out to the military to perform the most arduous tasks.*

*Note that only the men do the dancing. Their coverings are made of deer, rabbit, and sea otter skins. They have decorated their capes, and headdresses with feathers. The spears were seldom used for war, often in dancing.*

game for any miner or farmer who looked down the sights of his rifle and saw a native within range. No estimate has been made of the number killed, but the troops were not withdrawn until 1865. In the winter of 1858-59 ninety troops killed an estimated ninety Indians, and not all were males. In another action in February, 1860 nearly 300 Indians died. At least half were women and children.

This chapter describes "tribes" as family groups who shared a common language. They were not groups who lived and worked together. Each family group generally kept its independence, except when need required a larger group of people.

Almost fifty years after Fray Serra established the first mission at San Diego, a ship's doctor wrote his impressions of the California natives. The Italian, Paolo Emilio Botta in 1827 made these observations: "The men are of medium height, their skin a deep bronze color, their hands so small sometimes they don't fit in with the rest of their body. Their narrow foreheads and puffed out cheeks...they have little eyes which are always black...their nose is generally flat, wide at the base. The mouth is large and is usually adorned with very white and very straight teeth...they seldom have beards...(at the missions) nearly all speak Spanish. The Spaniards hate them...and mistreat them whenever they are able to do so."

The Italian's ship had touched at San Francisco (called Yerba Buena), Mission Santa Cruz, Monterey, Santa Barbara Mission, San Pedro (Mission San Gabriel), and San Diego.

"It is now about fifty years since the Spaniards have established themselves in that land, and have settled the Indians in their missions;...from that time on the depopulation has progressed...in the greater part of California...is at the present time almost deserted. [1827?] I heard from one of the missionaries that in his mission sixty marriages produced only eight children and of them only one survives now. Within twenty years if things continue...there will be only whites in California."

Horace Bell, a "ranger" in Southern California during the 1850s, 60s and 70s, published his views of the California Indians. Although he was noted for exaggeration, they reflected attitudes prevalent at the time.

"We will let those rascally redskins know they have no longer to deal with the Spaniards or the Mexicans, but with the invincible race of American backwoodsmen which has driven the savage from Plymouth Rock to the Rocky Mountains, and has herded him here on the western shore of the continent, and will drive him back to meet his kindred fleeing westward, all to be drowned in the Great Salt Lake."

Ranchers sometimes banded together to seek vengeance on starving natives who had butchered a calf to allay their hunger. All their lives the natives had relied on the land for their sustenance, but now the ranchers had run them off. Their source for gathering seeds, bulbs, roots and acorns was gone.

Armed ranchers in Humboldt County, for example, after dark were known to have settled in a ring around a slumbering Indian village. At daybreak they awoke the villagers with a single shot. As the drowsy natives came out into the open to see what had occasioned the gunfire, the ranchers shot them down, men, women, and children.

To be sure, only rare accounts of these murderous raids on the California Indians were ever publicized. Nevertheless, a rare few are on record in newspapers of those days. Here are two examples of what was printed.

### Sacramento Daily Union, June 11, 1863

"Five Indians were found suspended to a hydraulic flume, at Helltown (Butte Co.). The Indians have been suspected of committing several depredations lately, robbing cabins and running off horses. The 5 Indians were captured, bound and held as prisoners for 2 or 3 days by the citizens. It is not known whether they confessed to any crime, but it is certain the "Captain" and 4 of his tribe suffered the extreme punishment of Judge Lynch."

### Yreka Semi-Weekly Union, March 26, 1864

"The new military commandant of the district, Col. Black, is doing good service in Indian hunting. He keeps his troops in the mountains most of the time scouting, and has introduced a new method of treating hostile Indian prisoners—hangs them all. That style of dealing with a murdering Digger is very effective, and meets with universal approval by the citizen inhabitants of the hostile region. It seems to be a general sentiment here that a mean "Digger" only becomes a "good Indian" when he is dangling from the end of a rope, or has an ounce of lead in him."

Due in great part to the cholera, measles, and other epidemics of the 1830s their numbers dropped to about 4,500 in 1852. By 1856, only 3,000 remained alive, and by 1910 the number had dropped to 670. In 1930 they numbered only 763 statewide.

California State University, Humboldt

*Hupa Indians at a Yurok town on the Klamath River preparing to dance the Jumping Dance. They wear woodpecker-scalp headbands and carry tubular baskets filled with straw so as to keep their shape. Both this dance and the White Deerskin Dance gave the performers a chance to display their finery and wealth. An albino deer skin without a blemish changed hands for about $200 and attracted admiration.*

# Central California Missions

Monterey, except for its unique position as the only port-of-entry in Northern California, was a typical Spanish frontier pueblo. While governed by civilian councilmen and a council, it had a mayor, and its final arbitrator the *alcalde*, a judge.

The purpose of the Catholic Church missionaries was to bring the "heathens" to know Christianity and thereby save their souls.

Also interested in the success of missions was King Charles of Spain. He expected the mission fathers to "tame" the natives. Then as soon as they were Christianized, civilized and self-supporting, his missions would grow into pueblos. At that time, his plan was for the mission churches to become parish churches and the missionaries would become parish priests. The natives by this time would be producers, manufacturers of goods, or farmers, suppliers of food. In either case the natives would be earning tax revenue for the King's realm.

In addition to the religious and civil governments of each

California mission and pueblo, an independent military garrison gave protection from whatever sources might threaten the inhabitants. Mariano G. Vallejo of Sonoma was the commander of all the military forces in Northern California

In all Spanish explorations, a padre accompanied each one. The Franciscan Order supplied the personnel for the California campaign. The zeal to bring Christianity to the Indians could not have been better lead by a more dedicated and earnest leader than Father Junipero Serra. Walking from Baja California on an injured limb, Serra hobbled and was half carried to the first mission, in San Diego on July 1, 1769.

Hardship was nothing new to Serra. His difficult voyage from Cadiz, Spain to Vera Cruz, Mexico took 99 days. There he refused transportation to Mexico City. He insisted on walking the approximate 300 miles with one companion. They started out with no provisions, relying solely on providence and the goodness of the people they met on the way.

Serra founded his first mission in northern California, San Carlos Borromeo at Monterey on June 3, 1770. Later he relocated the mission buildings to a site overlooking the Carmel River, about five miles south.

Serra dedicated his next mission in the presence of a solitary Indian on July 14, 1771. He dedicated it in honor of San Antonio de Padua. Today the site's closest neighbor is the village of Jolon, eighteen miles south of King City. "The fifteen days that Father Serra remained (there) were days of intense joy." Father Serra's

(continues on page 25)

Museo Naval Collection, Madrid. Univ. of California Press

*The reception of Count Jean François Galaup La Perouse at Mission San Carlos Borromeo at Carmel in 1786 honored the first foreign visitor to come to California since Francis Drake came in June, 1579. This is also the first picture of California Indians by an artist who saw them. Father Fermin Francisco Lasuen, Serra's successor is standing in the doorway of Mission Carmel's fifth church (1783-1793). Note the three Indians pulling the cords of the Mission bells, to the right of the chapel. One can't help wonder at the first in the line of the Indians: a horse. La Perouse wrote this about the event: "before we entered the church, we crossed a square, where the Indians of both sexes formed a line; but their countenances showed no sign of surprise at our arrival, and even left it doubtful whether we should become the object of their conversation during the remainder of the day."*

*The façade of Mission Dolores Church in San Francisco.*

priests baptized and enrolled 158 natives in two years. In 1800 the neophyte population reached a peak of 1,118. In 1787 the church was considered the best in all of California. In 1805 it gained its highest population, 1,296 Indians. However, the top soil was too thin. Most of the land near the mission ultimately experienced a substantial loss in crop production. Today the fields are barren. All is silent and deserted.

The first vessel to enter San Francisco Bay, the *San Carlos* arrived in 1775. One year later Father Serra's assistant established the mission by the Golden Gate. The first building erected was the Presidio headquarters, built of adobe brick. Today an adobe brick section of the building's walls are still standing and form a part of the Officers' Club in the San Francisco Presidio. Adobe bricks are also in the mission church built several miles to the south of the fort.

The foggy and wet weather at Mission Dolores (San Francisco de Asis) caused the death of many Indians. Seeking a drier climate than the misty days about the mission, Padre Lasuen established the Mission San Rafael in 1817.

By 1830 only 219 neophytes populated Mission Dolores. Fifteen years later (1845) so few lived there that the then governor, Pio Pico, threatened to declare the mission abandoned.

The political turmoil created by the new city nearby, so overwhelmed Mission Dolores and the derelict fort that they, virtually in fact, had already been abandoned or secularized.

One writer commented in 1905, "Poor, sad Dolores! How

utterly lost it now looks, surrounded by parvenue (one who is not accepted socially…) buildings of pretentious greatness, and led up to by pavements and cement sidewalks. It is forlorn and neglected. The tiles on its roof and ridges are irregular and un-even. The wood cross on the front is old and staggering…"

Caring San Franciscans have since rebuilt Mission Dolores and now show it off to visitors to their city with pride.

Mission Santa Clara de Asis was located midway between Monterey and Mission Dolores in January 1777.

Father Fermin Francisco Lasuen succeeded Fr. Junipero Serra as Father President upon the latter's death in August 1784.

Lasuen next established Mission Santa Cruz in 1791. It was here that the second priest was martyred. He frequently disci-plined his neophytes by thrashing them with a metal-tipped whip. The natives suffered only long enough to strengthen their resolve of take revenge. Today nothing remains but memories of the Mission of the Holy Cross.

Also in 1791, Fr. Lasuen chose a site, named Soledad by those Spaniards who came from Mexico with Anza on his second trip. Here on October 9, accompanied by Padres Syar and García in front of a few natives, he raised the cross, blessed the site, said mass, and founded the Mission of Nuestra Señora de la Soledad.

For the following six years Fray Lasuen conserved his ener-gies by not establishing any new missions. In 1796 the new gov-ernor of the province, Borica, approved the founding of five more.

In 1797 Fray Lasuen left Mission Dolores for the establishment of Mission San José. At first a wooden structure with a grass roof served as a church. Adobe bricks formed the walls of the church when it was rebuilt over the next several years.

The next site was known as San Benito. In June 1797 the record gives credit to "Corporal Ballesteros (who) erected a church, missionary house and granary." Lasuen and Fathers Catalá and Martiarena dedicated the Mission to San Juan Bautista.

The last mission to be built in California was San Francisco Solano at what soon became Pueblo Sonoma. The first ceremonies took place on July 4, 1823. Nine months later, the mission church was dedicated. By the end of 1824 a big church of adobe

Courtesy Geo. Wharton James

*Dedicated on June 28, 1797, Mission San Juan Bautista reached a peak population with 1,248 souls in 1823.*

Courtesy Geo. Wharton James
*The Mission San Francisco Solano was the most northerly in the chain.*

brick, with a tile roof, a granary, and eight houses for the use of soldiers and padres were functional. The Indians at the mission came from 35 family groups.

Six years after the Indians completed the buildings, the mission herds totaled more than 8,000 cattle, sheep, and horses. Their grain crop yielded an average of nearly 2,000 bushels each year.

The missions were secularized in 1834-35. A clearer meaning of what happened came from the words: disestablish, purge, liquidate, or suspend.

Authorities in Spain had never planned to support the padres forever in their effort to save souls. They apparently believed after the second mission followed the first, so the third could furnish what the next one needed, and so on ad infinitum.

Such was not always the case. Drought often reduced a

28

mission's grain reserve to a dangerous level. Still, almost every new mission could count on the gift of several hundred cattle, enough to start a herd, from missions on either side of it.

But the self-help goal was never achieved. The Mexican Government was always so short of funds, only the help of wealthy Mexican citizens who volunteered gifts of endowments or gifts of income producing property to the Pious Fund of California made it possible for the missionaries to continue their work. The Fund paid an annual stipend of $22,000 to the padres of California. For the purpose of paying travel expenses for incoming and returning padres by land and sea, the Fund had a reserve of approximately $2,000.

The principal founders of the Fund were the Marquis de Villapuente de las Torres de Rada and the Marchioness de las Torres de Rada.

The Mexican Government virtually ignored their agreement to support the padres by paying them a regular salary. So when illegal traders offered to supply the padres with the goods they needed, hides and tallow were offered in payment. Ox drawn *carretas* and pack mules would usually deliver them to small boats which could load as many as 300 hides per trip.

Trading with the New England shipmasters was illegal since all California ports were closed to foreign vessels. Nevertheless a substantial commercial intercourse thrived between missions and ship captains.

In 1822 the ports of San Diego and Monterey were opened to

foreign vessels by Governor Sola. Custom duties were paid there on any cargo destined for California. It was then that regular visits by British as well as American trading ships were made with representatives calling on all the missions and presidios. Indian runners took invitations to mayordomos who were urged to come to the ship and select whatever they needed. Stocks usually included cloth, buttons, combs, cooking utensils, dishes, cocoa, cinnamon, oil, iron bars, and window glass.

At Mission Soledad on June 17, 1822, Father President of all the missions, Mariano Payeras, wrote to each mission authorizing them to enter into trading contracts as each might wish.

Annually traders would come to pick up the tallow and hides. The tallow was usually consigned to Lima, Peru. The hides were delivered to New England or Europe.

By an order dated October 24, 1842, the President of the Republic of Mexico ordered the Pious Fund liquidated and the proceeds turned over to the public treasury. Approximately $2,000,000 were thus seized by Mexico.

Further, from the highest authority in Mexico City the padres were told to distribute the livestock among their natives and to turn the Indians free.

Most padres complied, some remained at their abodes and others left the country. Virtually at every church the natives left and many took with them tools, animals, and in some cases works of art and even books from the libraries. It was easy for the natives to convert whatever they took into money for gambling or for buying drink.

A great many sank from bad to worse until only a few of the *rancherías* remained. Where there had been probably 30,000 in contented settlements under the rule of the padres, now neglect of the mission buildings began and ended when roofs caved in and walls crumbled to dust.

As for the stocks of grain, hides and tallow in warehouses, civil officials gave orders for traders to take as much in payment as they had agreed to give for merchandise ordered. Thus ended the cycle of looting.

*The old Russian Church at Fort Ross was restored in 1974 by the California Division of State Parks*

# Fort Ross

The first discovery which turned Russians in the direction of California took place when Admiral Behring of the Russian Navy discovered the northwest coast of America in the 16th century. Almost as important was Behring's report that he had also discovered the habitat of the fur seal.

Rumors of his two revelations found their way from St. Petersburg to the European capitals of Madrid and London. The result of the news reaching London ultimately led to the outfitting of Captain Cook's voyage of discovery to the north Pacific Coast. Likewise, the King of Spain ordered a similar expedition be sent from Mexico to lay claim to the land as far north of California as it found reasonable.

While the two expeditions did finally meet at Nootka on Vancouver Island, the Russians were moving ahead with a visionary plan of their own. They chartered a commercial enterprise, the Russian-American Fur Company, under the command of an enterprising adventurer and a man of great executive ability and energy named Shelekof. He chose for the head of the monopoly in the field, Alexander Baranoff, who had gone to Siberia in 1780.

One of Baranoff's early accomplishments was building the first vessel made from American timber to be launched (1794) from the northwest coast. The Russian-American Fur Company had Aleut Indians taking fur seals and otter pelts for them, in as many camps as they could establish along the Aleutian Island chain. They also made a permanent settlement, Amchatka, on the north American coast.

However, the Russians never quite adequately kept their Aleut hunters supplied with food. In some years, only one supply vessel reached the settlements, and in others no ship at all arrived with food. The long periods of rain, overcast skies and only short periods of sunlight were not adequate for raising grain.

Chamberlain Resenof set sail from Sitka on March 8, 1806 bound for California on a trading voyage for his firm. Exactly what he had to trade is not clear.

Baranoff ordered Kuskof to sail south. He arrived at Bodega Bay on January 8, 1809 where he established friendly relations with the natives. Kuskof sailed away for Sitka on August 29, having spent almost eight months exploring a fifty mile stretch of the coastline.

Although he didn't find a land locked harbor, he found a good anchorage with good protection from summer winds. He further discovered a location of something over 1,000 acres with excellent soil, timber, water, and good pasturage. This is the place Kuskof planned to build the Russian settlement, about 16 miles by water north of Bodega Bay, called Mad-shui-mui by the Indians. As Russian people were generally referred to as the people of Ross, the site became known as Fort Ross.

When the colony was completed there were 95 Russians, including 25 boat builders. About 80 Aleuts, with 40 of their skin boats, set out to hunt otter and fur seals. The Russians prepared timber for several months. When all was ready, they recalled all the Aleuts, and they went to work building a fort and the necessary buildings to go with it.

In a few months they had a fortified village which mounted twelve cannon, later to be increased to 40. All was completed in September, 1812.

In January 1813, a Spanish officer named Moraga was sent to Ross and returned to the Presidio on San Francisco Bay on January 27. As a result of Moraga's report, delayed as it was, in 1815 Governor Arguello wrote a letter to Kuskof, stating by the Viceroy's order, the settlement at Ross must be immediately abandoned.

Early in 1818 the Russians traded some manufactured goods from their own shops for California grain. This was their first commercial intercourse.

All the buildings at Ross were made of redwood. The fort, a quadrangular enclosure, measured about 300 by 200 feet. It was built of heavy timbers eight inches thick and fifteen feet long. They were buried three feet in the ground, leaving them 12 feet high. Horizontal beams or plates surmounted the heavy vertical timbers to tie them all into an impregnable wall. They also built a seven-sided blockhouse on the north corner, built of timbers one foot thick. It was 25 feet in diameter and two stories high and had 14 port holes for cannon. The stockade had 20 port holes.

On the east corner, just inside the stockade, they constructed the 25- by 35-foot chapel surmounted by a belfry with a chime of bells and a dome. Inside the fort was the Commandant's

*The Russian Fort Ross circa 1820.*

house, the officers' quarters, barracks for the Russian employees, and various storehouses and offices. They had a windmill for grinding corn, a tannery, workshops, farm buildings, granaries, cattle yards, etc. The population at Ross averaged 200 to 400 persons. The Russians were the officers, chiefs of hunting parties, and mechanics. The Aleuts were the hunters and fishermen. The California Indians were the laborers and servants.

From 1812 to 1840 the Russians also kept an establishment at the Farallon Islands near San Francisco. Their primary purpose was to capture seals. They took 1,200 to 1,500 skins annually. After 1818 the seals became scarce and only about 500 could be taken each year.

The five or six Aleuts at the islands killed 5,000 to 50,000 gulls annually and about 200 sea lions whose meat was salted for use later. The skins were used for making boats, and the bladders were made into watertight sacks for shipping the oil. The oil was used in cooking and for burning in lamps.

Agriculture was an important industry. The company had about 2,000 cattle, 1,000 horses and 1,000 sheep to use at Ross or to export to Sitka.

The Californios frequently requested articles made of wood, leather, or metal. The Russians even built several boats for Spanish officers and priests. Pine pitch was exported to Sitka in barrels.

Kuskof, the head of the colony, died in 1821. Karl Schmidt succeeded him but then Schmidt died only two years later.

In 1828 Duhart Cilley, a Frenchman who was making a tour around the world put in at Ross. He reported finding all the luxuries found in Europe there, while they were unknown in other parts of California.

Russian vessels continued to call in at Yerba Buena, as San Francisco was then called, two or three times each year from Ross or Sitka, with goods to trade for grain.

Meanwhile the Aleut hunters had decimated the sea otters north of Monterey. As a consequence the shipment of skins virtually stopped.

In 1839 the military governor of the northern province, Mariano G. Vallejo, warned his Mexican government of dangers which should be expected from the Russians.

Simultaneously, the Russian-American Fur Company decided to abandon Ross after 31 years there. The Hudson Bay Company considered buying the improvements and livestock for $30,000 but decided against it.

Next, the Russians, eager to get out, offered to sell everything to Vallejo for the same price and he too declined the offer.

In September, 1841 the Russians concluded a contract to sell everything to John Augustus Sutter. He had no cash to pay them, but they accepted Sutter's promise to pay in installments, with no down payment. Most of the livestock and movable property were moved to New Helvetia, at the confluence of the Sacramento and American Rivers, now the site of the City of Sacramento.

# Fort Ross

The colonists left their establishment at Ross in January 1842. John Sutter never did honor his promised installment payments.

More than 100 years of rain and wind on the open coast took their toll of the structures at Ross.

The State of California acquired the fort in 1906. The remaining buildings, the Greek Orthodox chapel, the Commandant's quarters and the stockade have been restored. The chapel, destroyed by fire in 1970, was reconstructed in 1974.

From Life in California, New York, 1846

*By the early 1840s, Yerba Buena began to assume the proportions of a town. This view looks eastward from the hills behind the hamlet to Yerba Buena Island and across the bay. Hide ships and coasting vessels are at anchor in the bay. The drawing was made in 1842 by Fred Henry Teschemacher who arrived in California in 1842 and was clerk and supercargo of a Boston hide trader until 1848.*

*John Marsh*

# The First U. S. Immigrant Landowners

The two earliest men to come from the United States and make their homes in the north were John Marsh and John Augustus Sutter. Both reached northern California ten years before Marshall found his golden pebbles.

John Marsh came first. He left Minnesota in 1836. He started a two-year course in medicine from an army surgeon at Fort Snelling, Minnesota. Unfortunately, the man died after one year, leaving his student Dr. John Marsh free to go where he wished.

He rode from Fort Snelling to Santa Fe, then through Yuma, Arizona to San Gabriel (later Los Angeles).

Inquiring about the possibility of taking up land, he learned that unless he became a Catholic and a citizen of California it was out of the question. He rode north from San Gabriel, and the farther north he rode the better the land looked to him, and water eventually appeared in creeks, streams, and rivers.

Marsh followed the San Joaquin River north until that river

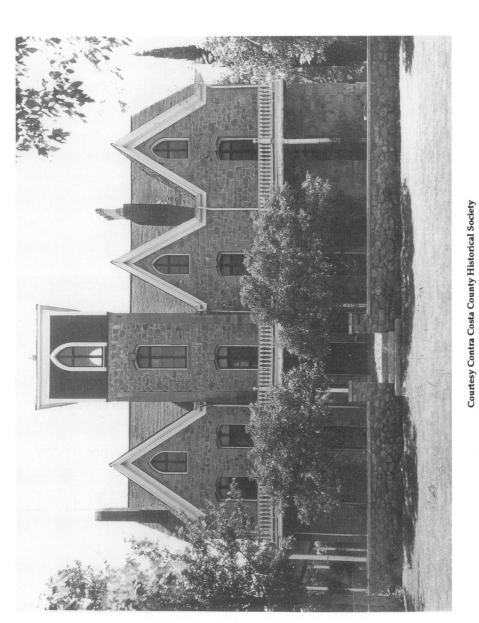

**Courtesy Contra Costa County Historical Society**

*Before he built his three-story stone mansion, John
Marsh lived a simple life in his adobe hut, on his 17,712
acres while his cattle herd increased year after year.*

joined the Sacramento. There as luck would have it he met José Noriega who had recently received a grant of 17,712 acres from the governor of the province. But, he said, "The mosquitos! The place is so remote too!" He wanted to sell and Marsh wanted to buy. They had a deal. Whether it was for 500 pesos or $500 is beside the point. Noriega took whatever it was and went away happy. Marsh had what he wanted and he too was happy. The year was 1837. He was the only settler and landowner in either the San Joaquin or the Sacramento Valley.

For eighteen years Marsh doctored the ailing Californios and took for his fees hundreds if not thousands of head of stock. Thousands of cattle grazed on his 17,712 acres. He regularly sold hundreds at a time to wholesale butchers from Sacramento and Stockton to Oakland and San Francisco. They paid him as agreed: in gold coin the day they picked up their cattle.

The Doctor made one such sale in September 1856. That afternoon he dressed for San Francisco, rode away to take the afternoon boat from Martinez, with a sack of gold between his feet.

Within a mile of his destination horsemen made him stop, pulled him from his buggy, and stabbed him to death.

Three disgruntled vaqueros who had worked for Marsh were apprehended but not convicted.

John Augustus Sutter came next. This Swiss native found himself in Missouri in April 1838. California beckoned him but the southern trail, fraught with danger from Apache and Yuma

Indians, was the route to be avoided if at all possible. He chose the
northerly trail, to the Columbia River, down it to the British built Fort

**Courtesy William J. Duffy**

*Captain John Sutter, the Swiss-born adventurer, quick
to recognize the potential of the Sacramento Valley, ob-
tained grants from the Mexican government, and established a land barony of his own in the heart of the
great valley.*

Vancouver.

Once at the Fort he awaited news of any ship going south to California. However, the first vessel which sailed down the Columbia headed for Hawaii, and Sutter was on it. He stayed in the islands for five months and then with a party he had recruited, sailed for Sitka, Alaska. His group consisted of eight Hawaiin men, two with wives, five white men, and himself. They reached Sitka but left there one month later. When they sailed into San Francisco Bay they were desperate for food and the vessel was leaking badly.

The Mexican officials at Yerba Buena denied them landing privileges. Told they must enter California only at Monterey, they sailed out and did make a landing at that port, hungry but thankful to be allowed to land. One condition permitted them to stay there. Sutter asked if he could settle in California. The ambiguous answer was, "you may stay if you apply for land east of any settlers who have grants from the government."

Sutter and his party went northeastward and chose to stop at the junction of the American and Sacramento Rivers.

His neighbors, Maidu Indians, were friendly. In due time Sutter put them to work, first making adobe bricks, and later putting up the walls of his storehouse, dwellings, kitchen and a series of shops. Around it all they built an adobe wall eight feet high with only one opening for a gate.

As time went on Sutter's welcome to companies of families coming over the Sierra Nevada mountains into California made him favorably known, and added to the numbers who made their homes near Sutter's Fort.

After the gold discovery, so many people squatted on his acreage that he lost control, though he never denied them the privilege of living on his land. Ultimately, these folks requested title be given them, and it was. No one compensated Sutter, and by 1852 the City of Sacramento had grown over his property and no local redress was ever offered.

Sutter gave up hope at the State Capitol and moved back to Washington, D.C., where he haunted the halls of Congress. His entreaties there were just as futile as they were at Sacramento. In poor health and without any income, only the memories of the wealth he once had in California were his constant thoughts during his last days. He died in Washington, D.C., in 1880. He was buried in a public cemetery in Lititz, Pennsylvania. His place in history is but a few lines in the history of California.

*Sutter's Fort in 1847*

# Bear Flag Revolt

When Brevet Captain John Charles Frémont returned from Oregon in early June, 1846, he led a detachment of topographical engineers to the Sutter Buttes.

That was far enough for word to spread around the Sacramento Valley that there were United States troops ready to seize California from Mexico.

From Sonoma down to Monterey about sixteen American residents, sympathetic to the rumor, hurried north to Frémont's side.

At the same time Don José Castro, leader of the Mexican forces at Monterey, feeling the danger from Frémont, sent a plea to General Vallejo at Sonoma for 200 horses. With that many more cavalrymen he reasoned he could successfully defend his capitol.

Vallejo turned over the requested horses to Castro's secretary who brought the message, a man named Arce, and a lieutenant, Francisco Alviso, and eight privates.

They planned to cross the Sacramento River near Sutter's Fort. They took the horses by way of Murphy's Ranch on the Consumnes River. There, fourteen resident Americans blocked their way, drove the escort away and took the horses for themselves.

*Gleason's Pictorial Drawingroom Companion*

*A native Californian, 1851.*

The Americans, by force of arms, had taken property of the Mexican Government. This was an act of war.

Taking the offensive on June 14, Frémont sent 33 men to capture Sonoma. This was another act of war on his own initiative. There was no resistance. General Vallejo received his captors as he would guests to his home. They took seats in his parlor and he ordered brandy for his visitors.

Vallejo asked, "by whom am I being taken prisoner?"

That stumped the spokesman for some minutes. He conferred with some of his fellow leaders. They agreed on the answer, "by the Republic of California." Surely no other republic was formed with less debate.

William Ide, an ex-school-master, assumed a position of leadership when he issued a procla-mation an-nouncing the

*From an early print*

*John C. Fremont*

birth of the Republic. Another of the insurrectionists, William Todd, a nephew of Mrs. Abraham Lincoln, decided to make a flag.

Todd asked for colored cloth suitable for his purpose. The wife of one revolutionist gave him her chemise and the wife of another contributed a petticoat. Todd completed the flag but forgot to include the "i" in the last syllable in California. At any rate, now the Republic had its flag.

With those details settled, the prisoners, Vallejo, his colonel and a captain, mounted their horses and followed their captors to Sutter's Fort.

Frémont, undoubtedly uncomfortable with his precipitous action taken without approval by any higher authority, sent a rider with a message to Commander Montgomery of the U.S. sloop *Portsmouth* anchored in Monterey Bay.

Next, Frémont told Commander Ide at Sonoma to request a keg of powder from the naval force now in San Francisco Bay. Instead of going for it himself, he sent two of his recruits, Fowler and Cowie. On their way the two ran into a pair of excitable Mexican horsemen. The riders killed both the Americans.

On May 31 the war with Mexico was announced, the new Republic a fact.

HMS Blossom *while anchored at Monterey in 1846, before the arrival of the squadron of three United States warships.*

# The Gold Rush

One of the biggest parades in a mass movement of people began on January 24, 1848. Several days before, James W. Marshall leaned down and picked up pebbles of gold in the stream bed under John Sutter's newly completed sawmill on the American River at Coloma, California.

Marshall, a millwright, working for the owner of an eleven league grant of land, couldn't keep a secret any better than the owner.

Soon the words, "gold on the American River!" echoed in every public place in Yerba Buena. Every ship leaving California carried letters exclaiming, "gold, men are picking it up in creeks—they don't even have to dig for it!" Newspapers in the eastern states displayed bold headlines screaming "gold! gold! in California!"

A trickle of people flowed across the continent, some riding horseback, others driving a team of horses pulling an overloaded

*Sutter's Mill at Coloma, where James Marshall found the nuggets on January 24, 1848, which triggered the Gold Rush.*

wagon. Thousands came around Cape Horn, many in boats ill equipped for a three month voyage, through some of the roughest oceans in the world. The passengers came from all walks of life. It was unlikely any had ever mined before they reached the American River. But they had read that men were picking up nuggets like they might pick up fallen fruit.

Meanwhile back in California some men were deserting their posts. Even the local military posts were being abandoned. Sonoma had 26 deserters, San Francisco lost 24, and Monterey the same.

**Marshall Gold State Park**
*His pick and shovel behind him, his feet in water, the man is panning for gold.*

However they came, on horseback or by ship, they knew they had been in a struggle. Now they struggled more. They had come to a country where meals were served only in towns, not in mining camps.

Provisions could be bought in a few places if one could walk that far. A shovel which cost one dollar elsewhere, would cost $10 along the Feather and American Rivers. The same was true of the price of a mining pan. It was not unusual to see a man working with a skillet or even a laundry tub to pan for gold.

Prospectors expected to pan for gold in the early years along the creeks with a pan of stamped iron, flat bottomed, with sloping sides, three inches deep and about 18 inches across at the top. They expected to dig up gravel-rich earth, throw it in their pan and soak it well with water. Then they would pick out the rocks and with a whirling motion create a circular current in the pan which would result in the lighter sediment spilling out over

*Marshall Gold State Park*

*Lunch time at the diggings.*

the pan's edge. Hopefully, whatever gold, if any, would have settled to the bottom. Unfortunately, panning required the prospector to kneel down with his feet often in water. If he stooped down or squatted to create the eddy in his pan, he just traded one uncomfortable position for another.

A less fatiguing method than panning was the use of a rocker or cradle. Then the miner would make a wooden hopper and set it over a canvas apron to feed water which emptied into an open trough about four feet long, with cleats running crosswise. The whole would be set on rockers so it could be given a rough, cradle-like agitation. Often one man shoveled in the soil while his partner bailed in the water. Regardless of which method they used, their hands and feet were in cold water for hours.

The flow of water diminished considerably in summer. At such a season miners would often turn a small stream away from its accustomed course by building a wing dam. Thus the diverted stream bed could be worked for the gold which might have been caught over eons in the gravel bed.

The tom came next. It really was an improved rocker. It was improved by virtue that it was kept in one position, and could not be rocked. It would be built where a steady stream of water ran through it. One man could operate the tom, shoveling in the soil. No one had to bail water or rock the frame. A miner would glean it only once a day, where the pan needed to be examined after every shovelful.

For everyone who found enough of the precious metal to

pay for his food, clothing and shelter, probably scores if not hundreds quit before getting back what it cost to get there.

Many former farmers went back to farming. Teachers taught wherever anyone opened a school. Former merchants tried to get jobs working for the few businesses in San Francisco and San Jose.

Nevertheless, some arrivals did strike it rich. Letters home told of their successes, encouraging some well-established heads of households to drop their occupations and head west. Some bought land, others sent back east for merchandise they knew they could sell on a market where little was manufactured.

*Marshall Gold State Park*
*Five Chinese men work with "company" of miners..*

*A one-man rocker.*

As an example, Hubert Howe Bancroft, so well-known at the end of the century for his vast library, tried for over three months to get work. Unsuccessful in 1852, he took a boat for Crescent City where he found work as a bookkeeper. Part of his compensation was the privilege of sleeping in his employer's store, which remained his only lodging for the year he spent there.

Bancroft eventually ordered books and stationary from the east. His first consignment was three cases, each shipped on a different sailing vessel. Only two arrived. With that stock he opened a store in a warehouse on Clay Street in San Francisco. His name remains known far and wide more than one hundred years later for his collection of historical material on the western states.

*Two black men working the "diggings". One is by the wagon.*

# Statehood

While one British naval vessel swung at anchor in Monterey Bay in July 1846, three United States warships warped their way closer to shore before they came to their moorings.

Commodore Sloat sent Captain William Mervine ashore with 250 U.S. Marines from the *Cayune*, *Savannah* and the *Levant* to demand the surrender of the city and its crumbling fort. Sloat promised the citizens the right to free elections and the privilege to practice any religion they chose.

No resistance met the naval force. In effect the Californios surrendered. On July 9, the residents of the pueblo Sonoma did likewise.

On July 23 Sloat turned over his command to Commodore Stockton who made his first duty the organizing of the California Battalion of Mounted Riflemen.

The lax civilian government of Monterey had consisted of an alcalde and a tax collector. On January 1847 a United States citizen, Thomas Larkin, replaced his Mexican counterpart as alcalde, judge and leader of the community.

Marines and sailors alike enjoyed the enthusiastic hospitality of Monterey. The Mexican-Californios would later be known far and wide as Californios. These people were showing their relief now that the uncertainty of which government would be responsible for their safety was settled.

Traders, waiting to import needed merchandise, now knew that contracts made under the approval of the new authorities, would be honored as written and not subject to duties made at the whim of a local Mexican appointee.

However, the discovery of gold nuggets in the mill-race of John Sutter's sawmill at Coloma by James Marshall upset whatever plans had been made for an orderly assumption of local government.

While not many Californios deserted their ranchos to seek the pebbles, flakes and dust of the yellow metal, a great many of the Americans on the spot in the early months of 1848 did leave. Even Consul Hartnell left behind his responsibilities at Monterey and went to the diggings. It was harder work than he thought. It seemed the earliest arrivals had picked up most of the loose nuggets. He returned to his post on Monterey Bay after a few weeks, better informed about the conditions in the mountains.

Ever since the Marines took control of Monterey, Mexican families hosted members of the fleet at dances. It gave the young ladies an opportunity to show off their yellow crepe shawls and their strings of California pearls, collected at Baja California. Many wore white lace mantillas. A rosary of carved amethyst adorned many a young lady's waist jacket. Young señoritas rode their horses wearing short skirts and small round hats.

Monterey awoke and was no longer a sleepy town. Grand caballeros rode their spirited horses to gay balls. They showed off their horses' silver studded trappings. Vaqueros, like their masters, wore wide-brimmed shiny black hats, coated with varnish. Caballeros wore black velvet trousers with spurs jingling at every move.

As in most of the incipient towns, San Francisco found itself with a population eager for more stability in its own government. Violence and crime, robbery and murder knew little control. Citizen meetings were held in numerous halls, calling for California to become a state.

Citizens gathered at torch-lit and mass sand lot meetings where passion and eloquence brought the answer to the question of statehood.

As a result, during the last ten days of 1849, five meetings were held in three locations where candidates were nominated and policies decided for the four districts represented: San Francisco, Monterey, Sacramento and San Joaquin.

The first political meetings were held in San Francisco on October 25 and 27, to vote on questions of adopting a state constitution, and to select candidates for State offices.

*Members of the first California legislature met in this building in San Jose in 1849 to conduct the business of the new state. The Fairmont Hotel occupies the site today.*

*This state capitol building was located at the foot of Georgia Street in Vallejo. Mare Island Channel is in the background.*

Also on October 25 in Sacramento, a measure passed which decided "to submit to the whole electorate the subject of selecting candidates to the people on the day of the (general) election. However, four days later at another meeting, a measure passed which said to nominate candidates "...without distinction (as to) party" for a legislative ticket for the District.

On October 30 at Monterey, a nominating committee of seven was appointed to name the candidates for that district.

Meanwhile, preparations had been made for the general election to be held on November 13. It turned out to be a very rainy day. Nevertheless, up and down the state, 12,872 votes were counted, and Peter H. Burnett was elected governor, John McDougal lieutenant governor, and George W. Wright and Edward Gilbert congressmen.

In December, at the first meeting of the state legislature, an act was passed calling for a statewide election to select county officers and a clerk of the supreme court.

Several facts of life appeared early in their first session and continued to plague the legislators for the first five years of the government. For the most part, they were large landowners accustomed to delegating chores to their employees or to their wives. Back home, the washerwomen kept their linens clean and the kitchen help prepared their food. Their wives saw to it that beds were supplied with warm bedding, and that the general comforts of home were taken care of.

Those comforts were greatly missed during their meeting at

San Jose.  In that winter of 1849 36 inches of rain fell between October 8 and March 22, and kept them damp and chilled.  They walked from their lodgings, through muddy trails and road, and to their place of work.  The city was unaccustomed to the crowd of delegates, the press, and the hangers-on who were seeking opportunities from the new government.

When the delegates' workday ended, almost to a man they moved to the closest bar to find comradery which they missed where they boarded.  They missed their wives and the warm meals they were so used to at home.  It is no wonder that the delegates kept the inner man so well fortified that they were known as the "Legislature of a Thousand Drinks."

Nevertheless, they worked hard, drafting a code of laws and dividing the State into 27 counties, and providing the means of revenue for the government.  They applied for statehood.

President Fillmore signed the bill approving the application on September 9, 1850.  The *U.S.S. Oregon* steamed into San Francisco Bay on October 18, with guns booming and flags flying, carrying the good news to California.

The discomforts of the first session were not severe enough to keep them away from the second session which opened on January 6, 1851 and continued until May.

Meanwhile, the largest land owner in Sonoma County, no longer a Mexican General, but by now Senator Mariano Guadalupe Vallejo, had been lobbying the members to move the capitol to the city of Vallejo.  He would contribute the land for a state capitol and $375,000 to erect a state house, governor's mansion, and whatever public buildings were needed.

Consequently, the Legislature voted to make Vallejo the permanent capital, and moved there for the third session on January 5, 1852. But there were problems. Wood to be imported from Hawaii had not yet arrived. The temporary building was unfurnished, boards were placed on stools, and nail kegs were in place for seats. As in San Jose, food was scarce, and there were no laundry facilities. They didn't like it.

Rooms were so scarce that 100 persons were forced to seek beds on the steamer *Empire* on which the northern delegates had arrived.

Within four days they voted to move the capitol to Sacramento. There they took over the Sacramento County Courthouse where they remained from January 1852 until adjournment in May 1852. Soon after they left, Sacramento was consumed by fire and in the same year was devastated by floods.

As a result, the legislature convened once again at Vallejo, on January 3, 1853, to begin its fourth session. Again, the weather was cold and blustery, and accommodations were little better than they had been the year before. They stayed one month.

The nearby town of Benicia, through its mayor, offered its City Hall as a capitol and offered to pay the expenses of the removal from Vallejo. The legislators gave the offer serious consideration. It was becoming obvious that Senator Vallejo could not keep his elaborate plans. As a consequence, on February 4,

1853, the governor signed a bill making Benicia the permanent capital, and the legislators met there on February 11. They remained one year and one week. At that time there were 27 Senators and 63 Assemblymen.

With a devious plan which worked, Sacramento business interests and politicians hired the paddle wheel steamer *Wilson G. Hunt*, loaded it with an ample stock of liquor and cigars, and sent it down to Benicia. There all the legislators were invited to a dinner and accommodations to spend the night.

The story of that night is that the party went on until almost every guest had retired, and then the *Hunt* left her moorings at Benicia and headed upstream. When the guests finally made their appearance the next morning, they saw the city of Sacramento. In any event, not enough, if any, complained. Thus Sacramento became California's State capital.

Fred Emanuels photo

*The Sacramento Capitol in 1995*

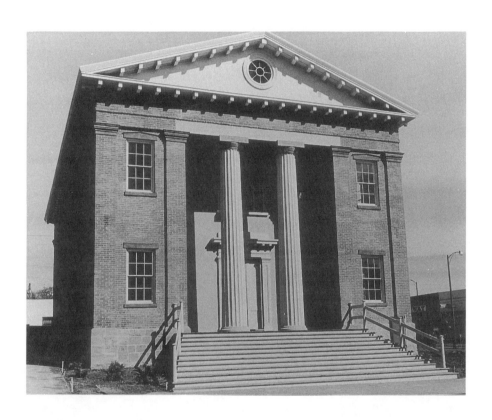

*The state capitol building in Benicia, formerly the city hall as it appeared in 1853 and as it still appears. The legislature met here for thirteen months from February 11, 1853 to February 4, 1854 before moving to Sacramento. The senators occupied desks on the first floor while the assemblymen climbed the stairs to their desks above.*

# Early Railroads

The very first use of a steam locomotive in California took place in San Francisco in the early 1850s. The growing city wished to extend Market Street west to Mission Dolores. However, sand hills 200 to 300 feet high blocked the way until dump cars were built locally and a steam locomotive was brought around from the east coast on a sailing ship. Once assembled, train loads of sand from 5th Street to 9th Street were dumped into the tidal swamp east of Battery Street and at the foot of Market Street. This reclaimed real estate soon became the site of

*Cowcatchers on locomotives were for the purpose the name implied: to catch cows and whatever livestock wandered on to the rails. An engine without a cowcatcher was easily derailed.*

scores of one-story mercantile establishments and eventually the city's wholesale produce district.

This work took place at the time placer miners were scouring every stream, creek and gulch panning for gold. Their every day need for existence depended on the stores with food and hardware near their camps.

In addition to food, everything such as cases of candles, ammunition, tools, barrels of horse shoes, bales of rope, and spirits left San Francisco on steam-powered river boats. Virtually all the cargo was unloaded at Sacramento where teamsters loaded all of it on to ox- or horse-drawn wagons. To the east, Folsom had become the distribution center where eight routes fanned out into the populated hills.

Winter and spring rains often delayed the loads in the relatively flat sandy country between Sacramento and Folsom. The heavily loaded wagons were especially vulnerable.

As time went on quartz mining began. These mines required cement, rails, ore cars, hoisting machinery, wire rope and pipe to name just a few of the heavy items. Delays to deliveries occurred frequently, which cost the mining companies heavily, and sometimes shut down their operation. Overloaded wagons or wet roads were most often the causes.

Theodore Judah, a young engineer with some experience in railroad building on the east coast, came to California and fortunately made his headquarters in Sacramento.

Judah recognized the need for rail transportation from riverboat to Folsom. The rolling terrain would be relatively easy

The "Pioneer", the first engine of the Sacramento Valley Railroad. It was called "Elephant" when it pulled the trains of sand in San Francisco.

*(upper) Sacramento Valley Railroad depot, shops, freight house at Folsom.
(below) SVRR freight house at Folsom*

to build through. Trains would make freight moving profitable. It would be exclusive and would permit no competition. And, just maybe, this 31 miles to Folsom would be the beginning of a transcontinental railroad.

He called on the owners of four of Sacramento's leading mercantile establishments: Leland Stanford, grocer; Collis P. Huntington, hardware merchant; Charles Crocker, dry goods merchant; and Mark Hopkins, hardware dealer.

The four agreed to finance his 31-mile line to Folsom and they incorporated it under the name Sacramento Valley Railroad. They bought the now-idled sand hauler locomotive from San Francisco and brought it to Sacramento on a barge pulled by a steam tug.

Judah established the line's shops at the Folsom terminal. Eventually the line needed more motive power; the expected freight hauling increased, and the company bought four more engines. Now, with their chief engineer's judgment confirmed, Judah convinced his four contributors to finance a railroad which would cross the Sierra Nevada and link up somewhere with the Union Pacific (which was to be built west from Omaha).

The four investors incorporated the Central Pacific Railroad of California on June 28, 1861. Judah accepted the post of chief engineer on a very modest salary.

The group enticed thousands of workers from Canton, China. Under Judah's direction they started building their line, not in the direction of Folsom but rather to Roseville.

The accomplishments of the laborers were of monumental

proportions. They chiseled granite, blasting rock under the most dangerous conditions, making a roadbed all the way up to 6,871 feet above sea level, with the almost primitive tools they had to work with. It was a task of monumental proportions. Hundreds died in the effort.

Once over the summit and down onto the Nevada desert, the laborers, under their Irish foremen, worked feverishly to lengthen the Central Pacific's tracks. For every mile of track laid, each company gained a greater federal subsidy.

In one 24-hour period the Chinese laid ten miles of rail.

The two competitors met in the desert of Utah, at Promontory Point on May 9, 1869.

While this link allowed trains to run from the Atlantic Coast to Stockton, California, it did not make the transcontinental railroad a reality.

Six months later, on November 10, 1869, the final link, from Stockton to Niles, was completed over the Altamont Pass, and thence to the ferry terminal at Alameda, making Judah's dream come true. A coast to coast railroad began operating.

Eight years of cutting through the Sierra Nevada taught the engineers the task they faced every winter, keeping the rails free of snow. They found they couldn't keep the trains running without more than the snowploughs they had available. As a solution, they decided to build roofs over the line in the most likely places for the snow to build up. Ultimately they had to build forty miles of snow sheds before they would know their job was done.

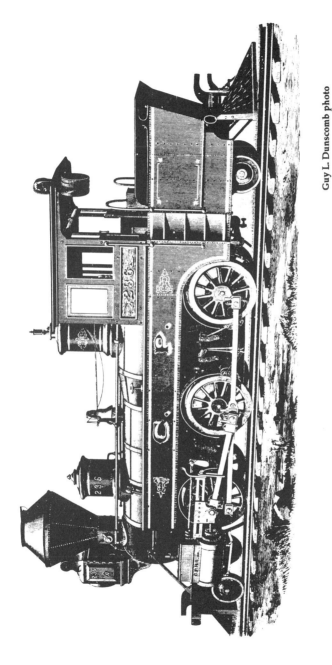

Guy L. Dunscomb photo

*Central Pacific's #236 was built under the direction of A.J. Stevens, Master Mechanic of the Central Pacific Railroad, at the Sacramento shops. This 2-6-2 tank engine was designed for suburban passenger service. Such heavy trains required powerful engines in the morning and evening rush hours for the run between Alameda and Oakland wharf, which extended two miles out in the bay, and this class of motive power was the result.*

*The wood-burning engine and coach have stopped at Marshall on Tomales Bay, approximately half way on its 93-mile run from Sausalito to Cazadero.*

# Early Railroads

Spurred on by the demand for redwood lumber by home builders on all sides of San Francisco Bay, North Pacific Coast Railroad started running trains in 1875 from Sausalito to Cazadero, about five miles north of the Russian River.

They built the narrow gauge line to pass through Point Reyes Station, then known as Olema Junction. It ran along the east shore of Tomales Bay and on to Monte Rio and Duncan's Mills. Several towns and numerous campgrounds sprang up along the right-of-way. In addition to hauling lumber, numerous dairies shipped their cream daily to the Point Reyes Creamery for churning into butter.

In summer, the wood-burning locomotives delivered hundreds of vacationers fleeing San Francisco's fogbound skies for the warm climate and the forest-shaded campsites in Marin and Sonoma Counties. Until 1917, on Friday and Saturday afternoons, two trains of ten passenger coaches each, full of travelers, required a pair of engines on the head end. On Sundays, the ten-car trains arrived back in Sausalito, one hour apart.

However, by 1920 the former vacationers were driving their own automobiles on the recently graded or paved county roads. Dairies delivered the cream themselves. The narrow gauge railroad suffered increasing difficulties when Northwestern Pacific Railroad built a standard gauge line along the Russian River to Cazadero, thus competing with the lumber shipped to the Bay Area. It also offered faster schedules from Sausalito to Monte Rio. The narrow gauge line along Tomales Bay carried no passengers at all after 1921, and occasionally ran with only one or two riders. It shut down in 1923.

### Tahoe-Truckee

When tourists came from San Francisco to visit Lake Tahoe before 1900, they left the Central Pacific train at Truckee. There they boarded a stage which took them over the Tahoe-Truckee Toll Road. It had been built in 1860 by John A. Huntington and remained a rocky, rutted, single buggy-wide trail. At what became known as Tahoe City, the passengers were left without a scheduled means of transportation to their destinations.

By 1900 so many travelers were stranded there that the Bliss family built a lodge, Tahoe Tavern, at Tahoe City.

The Bliss interests also replaced the stages running over the Toll Road with a narrow gauge railway. In early 1900 it started running its wood-burning locomotives sixteen miles, from Truckee to the Tahoe Tavern.

At the Tavern, a wharf had been built out into the Lake, and on it the trains terminated their trips. Passengers having a destination at one of the many resorts around Lake Tahoe, took only a few steps from the train to the steamer, the company's *Tahoe* or *Nevada*. Later, the firm acquired the side paddlewheel steamer *Governor Stanford*, which ran around the lake three days each week.

In 1926 the Bliss family leased their railroad to the Southern Pacific for $1 per year. The lessor immediately tore up the narrow gauge track and replaced it with heavier standard gauge rail. Passengers could now ride in the same railroad car from Oakland to Tahoe Tavern, where they would board a boat to take them to their final destination.

However, even this improvement in service couldn't slow the tide sweeping many sections of the country. By the 1920s people were buying their own cars and deserting the railroads. As a consequence, the Southern Pacific abandoned the Truckee to Lake Tahoe Railroad in 1942.

Since then, the State of California has replaced the tracks with a section of State Route 89.

CalTrans, Sacramento

*The Tahoe-Truckee train headed for Truckee*

*The S.S. Alexander Duncan with tanks fitted below deck, also carried crude from Ventura to Alameda Point in San Francisco Bay*

# Oil

The earliest use of petroleum in California comes from the record of Juan Bautista Anza's overland trip of exploration in 1775. In his diary, Padre Pedro Font notes the Indians' plank canoes that he saw in the area of what is today Carpentería in Santa Barbara County. "They are very carefully made of planks which they work with no other tools than their shells and flints. They join them at the seams by sewing them with very heavy thread of deer sinew, which they have, and fit the joints with pitch, by which they are made very seaworthy, strong and secure."

Font watched the natives at work. His "pitch" was tar which seeps from the hillsides in the area.

In Thomas O. Larkin's report, the U.S. Consul at Monterey reported in 1846 the use of bituminous pitch to cover the roofs of houses.

Some historians consider the beginning of northern

California's commercial production to be in Humboldt County. The first well was drilled along the Mattole River in 1865. A small amount of oil was shipped by sea to San Francisco.

By 1867 eastern kerosene was selling in San Francisco for less than it cost to refine and market California's small production.

In 1875 crude oil production statewide is recorded as 12,000 barrels. Fifteen years later, in 1890, the State produced 300,000 barrels a year.

In California, crude was refined at first by the "batch" pro-

Chevron Library Services

*From Rancho Ojai, the Pico Canyon Pool in Ventura County, a 2-inch pipeline carried crude oil to Newhall in 1879. Later, the line was later extended to Ventura where Pacific Coast Oil Company's two tankers loaded the crude oil for the refinery at Point Alameda in San Francisco Bay.*

cess. This began with a steel bowl, the still, large enough to take several barrels of the black crude (the "batch"). A fire was lit under the bowl which heated the crude and the light ends vaporized. A hood over the bowl collected the vapors and condensed them into liquids. After all the vapors were condensed, the tar-like residue was collected and sold to the city of San Francisco for paving streets.

By far the biggest demand for petroleum products was for coal oil, followed by grease. In 1865 California imported over a half million gallons of coal oil from Pennsylvania. It retailed for as much as a good dinner in a San Francisco restaurant or hotel: $1.70 per gallon.

A steady source of crude came to San Francisco Bay when a well on the Ojai Ranch in Ventura County sent its crude north in a two-inch pipeline to a waiting tanker anchored off the coast. There, the first ship to receive oil was the *Santa Cruz*, powered with a steam engine driving a single propeller. Several tanks had been fitted in the cargo holds. A second ship, the *Alexander Duncan*, almost a carbon copy of the *Santa Cruz*, alternated making weekly trips to the Pacific Oil Company refinery at Point Alameda in San Francisco Bay. This wooden hull ship, built in 1876 at the Risdon Iron Works in San Francisco, was 140 feet long, with a 25 foot beam.

The Standard Oil Company, Ohio, bought the Pacific Oil Company in 1901, after the California company moved from Alameda Point to the 118 acres it bought at Richmond for $15,000.

*From 1895 the S.S. George Loomis carried 6,500 barrels of crude oil per trip from Ventura to the Alameda Point refinery until 1901.*

During the time that the refinery at Richmond was being built, two noteworthy events took place. The first true tanker came down the ways. She carried about 6,500 barrels from Ventura on each trip. The *George Loomis* made her first voyage delivering crude to Richmond on June 1902.

The other outstanding feat was the completion of a pipe line by the Standard Oil Company from the southern San Joaquin Valley to Richmond. The first crude through that line reached Richmond on July 18, 1903.

Since then, other companies have built refineries around San Francisco Bay and pipe lines to feed them.

In 1893 the City of Los Angeles developed a successful oil burner to power its electrical generators. The same year, the Santa Fe and the Southern Pacific Railroad both began using oil, replacing coal, in their steam locomotives.

In 1906, the Pacific Coast Oil Company took on its parent's name, Standard Oil Company of California.

PACIFIC COAST OIL COMPANY

ALAMEDA POINT

CALIFORNIA.

REFINERY AT ALAMEDA POINT.

The Pacific Coast Oil Company paid $30,000 for eight acres of the western tip of what is now the Alameda Naval Air Station in 1880. Contruction of the refinery cost another $130,117. At that time the transcontinentel railroad, the Central Pacific, terminated its run along the north side of the refinery. Passengers then took the Alameda ferry to the Ferry Building in San Francisco.

# Earthquakes and Volcanos

To explain some of the reasons for California being shaken frequently by earthquake, several fundamentals should be explained.

A block of the earth's crust slides. This crust may be anywhere from twenty to forty miles thick under the continent. However, under the oceans the crust is a thin as four miles.

The crusts are called plates. They move as much as four inches a year.

Seismologists tell us there are only seven major plates around the Earth. Here, on the Pacific Coast, there are two which are moving. The Pacific Plate and the North American Plate are grinding against each other. The first is moving to the northwest, jostling northern California on its way to thrust itself under the south coast of Alaska.

As the giant plates move, they collide or pull apart, unleashing awesome earth-deforming tremors. Also, whenever a plate

*upper:* looking east on California Street from the Stanford home (extreme right) with the Fairmont Hotel (left)

*lower:* remains of City Hall

breaks off an edge of the other, we feel an earthquake. This chipping thus makes a fragment-size plate, of which there are many. One example of fragmentation is the Juan de Fuca Plate under the northwest corner of Washington State.

While erupting volcanos often start earthquakes, the reverse is also true. When one plate squeezes under the other, the one on top may rise even if it covers scores of square miles.

The surface evidence of plates colliding in northern California appears along what we know as the San Andreas Fault. This 600 mile long crack in the Earth's surface has helped form Tomales and Bolinas Bays in Marin County, and the Crystal Springs Lakes in San Mateo County.

Movement along the San Andreas Fault has been largely horizontal rather than up and down. That part of northern California known as the Point Reyes Peninsula, west of State Route 1, has been moving north, relative to the rest of Marin County.

Geologists explain that the soil of the Peninsula is unlike any other across the Fault. Further, they say that the only location of similar matching earth is along the coast of San Luis Obispo County, some 240 miles to the south.

At 5:13 am on April 18, 1906, beneath the sea, the Pacific Plate jerked its way north, rubbing the North American Plate. The Point Reyes Peninsula, on which the towns of Bolinas and Inverness stand, jolted northward eighteen feet.

In San Francisco, Police Sergeant Jesse Cook reported "there was a deep rumbling, deep and terrible, and then I could see it actually coming up Washington Street. The whole street was undulating. It was as if waves of the ocean were coming toward me, billowing as they came."

A few blocks away, at the San Francisco Examiner's city desk, John Barrett heard the same low moaning sound. He and his fellow workers found it difficult to keep their feet. "It was as though the earth was slipping away from under us."

Roy D. Graves Collection

*April 18, 1906, 2:30 p.m. By the time the fire burned down, the entire area in this photograph would be destroyed.*

The Sergeant reported, "trolley tracks were twisted, some pointing to the heavens, their wires down, wriggling like serpents, flashing blue sparks all around. The streets were gashed in any number of places. From some of the holes water spurted; from others, gas."

Everywhere noise. Screams nearby. More screams a block away "what happened?" Still in night dress, wandering men and women asked the question, "what happened?"

People were dazed, pale of face, many moaning, some talking to an invisible audience, all hanging on to something.

Horse-drawn fire engines, with bells clanging, and fires burning under the boilers for their steam pumps, drew up to the edges of burning buildings. Men pulled out their hoses but stopped at the cry from their mate at the hydrant, "there's no water!"

*Derailed train at Point Reyes Station, two miles from the estimated sixteen-foot dislocation of the earth. (Bruce A. Bolt, Director Seismographic Stations, University of California, Berkeley)*

There was no water in any hydrant but one in all of San Francisco. Later they understood. The water mains leading into the city from Crystal Springs Lake and from San Andreas Lake were ruptured by the quake.

Now the dark smoke mushroomed over the produce area and up toward Chinatown, fueled by dried out siding of the wood buildings. The little water stored in the city cisterns, from 20,000 to 90,000 gallons in each had been pumped futilely onto the flames by 9:00 am.

People carrying all they could started streaming down Mis-

*To the police and the military, the order was "Shoot to kill" all suspected looters. (Moshee Cohen)*

sion, Howard and Folsom Streets hoping to find a way to flee the burning city.

All over the city from Van Ness and Dolores to the west and from Townsend Street to the south, the survivors moved their bedding outside their homes and cooked and set up housekeeping outdoors, thankful to be alive. Golden Gate Park filled with residents who feared more shaking of their damaged homes.

All of San Francisco's fine hostelries were demolished if not by the quake, certainly by the fire. The Palace, the St. Francis, and the Fairmont Hotels were skeletons. Nearly every large office building died the same way.

Federal troops from the Presidio in San Francisco, and from other army and naval installations around the San Francisco Bay were ordered in to help the police stop looters and maintain order.

Buildings on the west side of Van Ness Avenue were dynamited in order to widen the city's already widest thoroughfare, to provide a firebreak. Flames devoured all the buildings along the east side of Van Ness, but they didn't jump across between Bay Street and Golden Gate Avenue.

In time, the fires burned themselves out, but fear of another big shake kept people satisfied to live in the city parks for weeks following the great Earthquake of 1906.

While the volcanos in northern California are slumbering now, they form a string of volcanos, most still active, which fan out from the Philippines in a semicircle up through Japan, the

Aleutian Islands, Alaska, and down through Washington, Oregon, California, Mexico and South America.

Mt. Shasta has an elevation of 14,162. It last erupted in 1786. Just 80 miles to the south lies Mt. Lassen, with an elevation of 10,453 feet, and last erupted with a mighty roar from the side of its crater on May 22, 1915. While further activity ceased in 1917, hot springs, fumaroles, and hot mud pots are still numerous.

*Mt. Lassen from Anderson, 50 miles distant, upon the eruption of Mt. Lassen, May 22, 1915. (Photo Myers)*

# Panama Pacific International Exposition

In planning for the San Francisco Panama Pacific International Exposition of 1915, fund raising began at a luncheon in the Merchant's Exchange Building in 1910. Forty four individuals each pledged $25,000. This was a large amount by 1910 standards.

The pledged seed money wasn't put to work right away, as the city was still rebuilding from the 1906 earthquake.

Californians wanted to celebrate the opening of one of the most difficult construction jobs in the world. Men had literally hacked their way through mosquito-infested jungles to make way for the Panama Canal. When finished, this achievement would cut down the distance cargo ships had to travel. On a one-way trip to New York, it would save 7,873 miles, and to Liverpool there was a 5,666 mile savings.

Only nine years after the Great Fire of 1906, San Francisco dredged mud from the bay and filled in 635 acres. It was a square

**Marilyn Blaisdell Collection**
*The 43-story Tower of Jewels*

mile of swamp which became the site of the last of the world's greatest expositions.

The boundaries of the exposition grounds were Chestnut Street on the south, Fillmore and Fort Mason on the east, the Presidio hills to the west and the bay wall on the north.

Before they could start construction, contractors tore down 200 buildings. They reserved the west end of the grounds for an automobile race track they would build later.

The men responsible dreamed dreams of what they wanted to show the world. Then they built their dreams in what became San Francisco's finest hour.

They built courts, fountains, and the biggest building in the world, the 1,000-foot long Machinery Building.

The elegant landscaping made room for 6,000 pansies, 10,000 veronicas, 5,000 junipers, and 30,000 trees.

Looking down on the Fair from the vantage point of Divisadero and Broadway, one could view a picture containing all the arts, the finest architecture and 1,500 sculptures. Many were originals, and several were by the French sculptor, Auguste Rodin. There were colorful scenes one would recognize from Asia, Rome and Greece.

Electricity made daylight out of night. A barge anchored off the Marina flashed 45 search lights, some in color, over the night sky above the fair.

All of this was happening when some of the visitors came from homes still without electric lights and without telephones.

They saw displays which revealed the essence of what would become their future.

People came. Those outside the San Francisco Bay Area came by train. No paved road yet existed from Portland, Oregon or from the eastern states across the plains and mountains and down the Sierra Nevada. From the East Bay, visitors could take a ferry boat directly to the grounds.

A multitude of visitors came by ship. In 1915, the Pacific Coast Steamship Company fleet furnished its passengers with luxurious accommodations on the *Governor*, *Congress*, and *President*. Their ships made regular runs between Seattle and San Diego with scheduled stops at San Francisco and San Pedro.

During the exposition the steamers *Great Northern* and *Northern Pacific* furnished through trips by rail from Chicago and by ship to San Francisco from the terminal at Flavel, Oregon, at the mouth of the Columbia River. The enormity of the exposition was theirs to stare at in wonder as the steamers came through the Golden Gate and slowed down as they passed the Palace of Fine Arts and the Tower of Jewels. The jewels were the more than 100,000 Austrian colored glass panels which fluttered in the wind and sparkled off mirror settings. At night, dozens of spotlights exaggerated the effect.

After the fair closed, fast travel from Seattle to San Diego was continued with the *H.F. Alexander* and the somewhat smaller *Emma Alexander*.

As if all of those vessels were not enough, two more ships

had arrived for that service in 1910. The *Harvard* and the *Yale* made round trips, alternately, four days a week. One would pull out of San Francisco about 5:00 pm, and the other departed San Pedro at the same time. Each reached its destination by 10:00 o'clock the next morning. Service ended with the collapse of coastwise shipping in general about 1936.

No radio or television station existed in 1915, but newspapers told the story, "San Francisco has done it. They have exceeded their dreams."

*James Earl Fraser's "End of the Trail" sculpture on the Court of Palms portrays Iroquois Chief American Big Trees*

*South Gardens, Tower of Jewels, glass-domed Horticultural Building*

People came for their first or tenth time in a jovial mood. They were happy. Nowhere else could anyone ever view a greater spectacle than the Panama Pacific International Exposition. As they came through the turnstiles ahead of them, they saw the Tower of Jewels, 435 feet high.

San Francisco showed the world with zest and with magnificent buildings of extravagant designs. Inside, some of the finest tapestries from Europe were hung, loaned to San Francisco in some cases for fear they might suffer or be stolen by an invading army in their homeland. In San Francisco they would be safe.

Before the contractors completed the Machinery Building, when only the two side walls and the roof were in place, Lincoln Beechey flew his pusher biplane through it in one of his

101

death defying stunts. A steam locomotive, set up on jacks, with fire in its fire box and steam driving the wheels, ran for all to see close up. Another locomotive, a new Pennsylvania Railroad electric 4,000 horsepower locomotive, was open for people to climb in. Everything was the biggest, the newest, the most awe inspiring.

The Court of the Universe, the Court of Abundance, and other courts were evidence of a changing and challenging world.

A centerpiece of the fair was the extravagant Palace of Fine Arts designed by Bernard H. Maybeck, one of the greatest architects active in the San Francisco area. It was full of paintings from the old world. People who would never get to Europe were bewildered, unable to believe their eyes. It featured 11,000 works of art, including paintings and sculptures. Here they saw what they had read about. Little did they know that San Francisco so appreciated this Palace that they would preserve it. Eighty years later it still stands in all its original setting, surrounded by a lagoon and floodlights.

The Festival Hall seated 3,500 persons. The soaring dome of the Horticultural Palace was the largest of its kind, taller than the Saint Patrick Basilica in Rome.

One building contained a working model of the Grand Canyon, and another contained an astonishing duplicate of Yellowstone Park, complete with an Old Faithful Geyser spouting and the Boiling Pots gurgling and bubbling.

In still another, people sat in a fifteen-row cone, which re-

Marilyn Blaisdell Collection
*The Palace of Fine Arts*

volved around a stationary working model of the Panama Canal. At every other seat a telephone receiver told the listener what was taking place in the model before him. Wireless antennas flashed sparks, sending messages to ships coming in.

The exposition grounds contained 47 miles of aisles. Operators drove small tractors pulling elephant trains. Visitors stayed on as long as they wished, the train stopping when passengers signaled. A ride cost 10 cents.

Author William Saroyan wrote of what he saw, "(this place) is a place that couldn't be real!"

In one building, the Ford Motor Company set up an assembly plant. During the 288 days of the fair they assembled 4,400 black Model T Fords.

On San Francisco Day 350,000 people attended, virtually the city's entire population. They paid $125,000 in admission fees. Now that they had seen it, no one doubted that San Francisco had earned the sobriquet, "The city that knows how."

Famed author Edward Markham wrote, "it is the greatest revelation of beauty that has ever been seen on earth."

The Liberty Bell was brought from Philadelphia that visitors might see America's symbol of freedom.

The bronze sculpture, The Thinker, by Rodin, made its temporary home in the Court of the French Pavilion. With France at war with Germany, it was safer here. Its permanent location would later grace the lawn in front of the Palace of the Legion of Honor.

Another feature of the exposition was a 65-acre zone where children played games, ate food, and in the case of the very young, spent hours under the care of a day care vendor. Candy shops offered their sweets, and every attraction that merchants could think of which would draw children was there. A white horse that could add and subtract figures amazed adults and children alike. The horse's handler asked the horse questions which required a number to answer. The horse stamped a hoof the number of times required for the correct answer.

When the Panama Pacific International Exposition closed, it left memories in the hearts and minds of a generation of people who would think to themselves that they were looking at the changes that have come to civilization before most people know they have been invented.

The exposition was a financial success. The profit from the fair paid for the construction of the civic auditorium in San Francisco, still in use eighty years later.

The Key System operated trains from San Leandro, Oakland, Piedmont and Berkeley to the Ferry Terminal located near the current Bay Bridge Toll Plaza. The ferry, Claremont, below, was one of the boats which connected with the trains and crossed the Bay every twenty minutes. A coffee shop catered to passengers.

# Transportation Comes of Age

The story of modern highways has its beginning in 1895. In that year, California, by act of the legislature, created the State Bureau of Highways and acquired the Lake Tahoe Wagon Road, a pioneer toll road, as the first state highway.

This first designated highway was typical of the main roads along the Pacific slope before the railroads came into existence. Grading of the toll road was spasmodic even though the Lake Tahoe Wagon Road required 50 men and 600 horses for the service from Placerville to Virginia City, Nevada. In 1862, 30,000 tons of freight and 36,500 passengers traveled over this mountain road.

Under the Act of 1895, the legislature empowered the governor to appoint three men to the Bureau of Highways. These three bought a team of horses and a buckboard wagon and drove into every corner of the state, covering 7,000 miles.

The commissioners' report of November 25, 1896 included a

map of a proposed state highway system which set the main features of the system that we have today.

In 1921 the principal highway from San Francisco to New York was the Lincoln Highway. It began in the parking lot of the Palace of the Legion of Honor in San Francisco. Its route included the Ferry Building, where motorists would take the only ferry which carried autos to Oakland, the Creek Route ferry. It came up the Oakland Estuary and docked at the foot of Broadway. Drivers would then take 14th Street, make a right turn and head out East 14th Street all the way to Hayward.

The Lincoln Highway then passed through the village of Dublin, along Main Street in Livermore, and over the Altamont Pass to Stockton, and on to Sacramento.

Drivers had the option of going to Reno via Carson City, or by way of Donner Summit. In either case they followed the Truckee River to Wadsworth, where they made a right hand turn to follow the signs to Fallon.

From there, the Lincoln Highway continued east to Ely and Salt Lake City, continuing on to Laramie, Cheyenne, North Platte, and on to New York.

In 1921, most of the road was unpaved. Even in many of the towns where "Main Street" received the designation, the Lincoln Highway had a crushed rock surface at best.

At the beginning of the 1920s, no bridge crossed over San Francisco Bay nor the Sacramento and the San Joaquin Rivers, below Sacramento and Stockton respectively.

Where the Bay and the two rivers needed a crossing, ferry-boats made transit possible.

To cross into San Mateo County from the East Bay, a motorist drove through downtown San Jose, or took a ferry from Oakland to San Francisco.

For motorists with destinations of Sacramento or further north, they crossed Carquinez Strait by ferry.

To travel across the Golden Gate, ferries ran from Sausalito to San Francisco.

The boats satisfied their customers except on Sunday nights

**Contra Costa County Historical Society**

*This long line of cars is waiting at the Rodeo ferry for the boat to take them to Vallejo. People who had never considered buying a car found that they could, in the early '20s when Ford sold his Model T five passenger touring car for $295 (without an electric starter and demountable rims).*

and on National Holidays. On those days, the boats, with their limited capacity, failed to convey the motorists to their destinations as fast as they came to the ferry slips. On Sundays a driver would not be surprised to find a long line of autos ahead of him. Waiting for the ferry often took two to four hours, especially on national holidays.

During the week, freight boats departed the San Francisco Embarcadero every afternoon for towns up the several rivers.

A boat with a destination of Napa had cargo on board for the towns all the way up to Clear Lake. The boat for Petaluma carried freight for that town as well as for Healdsburg, Sebastopol, Santa Rosa, and communities along the Russian River.

Retail merchants continually complained about the time it took for an order telephoned to San Francisco to be delivered to them if they were located north of the Carquinez Strait.

Two men in Vallejo, Aven J. Hanford, a grocery store owner, and Oscar Klatt, a wholesale grocery salesman, repeatedly discussed the problem and finally decided they could correct it.

First, in 1916 they incorporated the American Toll Bridge Company. Then they approached the State Division of Highways and offered to build a two lane bridge for autos and trucks from Antioch to Sacramento County, across the San Joaquin River. They proposed that if the state would allow them to keep the tolls they would construct it at their own expense.

It just so happened that the San Francisco Automobile Dealers Association had been buying full page advertisements in their

*A scow schooner with a load of hay. The steersman stands on a pulpit in the stern so as to see over the deck load.*

# SAFETY

## MOTORS MUST BE

## STOPPED AND ACETYLENE

## LIGHTS EXTINGUISHED

*Before electric headlights, signs such as this were posted on all ferries which carried motor vehicles. Acetylene gas occasionally leaked from the tubing which fed gas to the headlights, hence this safety measure.*

two major daily newspapers, the Examiner and the Chronicle. These ads deplored the status quo and implored the state to take the lead and build bridges wherever needed.

This kind of an appeal played right into Hanford and Klatt's hands. With that kind of urging, the state accepted their offer to build the Antioch Bridge. They built the bridge at a cost of $2 million and opened it to traffic in January 1926. Over the years, ships collided with the span and caused it to be closed for repairs in 1958, 1963, and 1970.

In December 1978, the State erected a new bridge at a cost of $34 million. It is called the John A. Nejedly Bridge, named for the once State Senator from Contra Costa County.

The American Toll Bridge Company sold additional stock in the company to finance the erection of a steel cantilever, three-lane wide structure over the Carquinez Strait. It cost them $8 million to build, and they opened it on May 21, 1927. In 1958, the state bought the bridge from its owners for $38 million.

A parallel span, also three lanes wide, opened in 1958. Thus the water barrier to fast transportation disappeared.

As late as the early 1960s, the highway, known as U.S. 40 between Vallejo and Sacramento, consisted of only two lanes. In towns like Fairfield, Vacaville, Dixon and Davis bumper to bumper traffic made the route a nightmare for commercial and private vehicles alike. To the south of Vallejo, U.S. 40 motorists in Oakland made their way north on San Pablo Avenue and its extension through Richmond, San Pablo, Pinole and Hercules.

(continues on page 117)

The completion of the Carquinez Bridge in 1927 should be remembered for its three accomplishments. First, private enterprise built the bridge, not government funding. Secondly, consider how much time each person making the crossing saves instead of waiting for a ferryboat. Thirdly, we should understand the unique method the engineers used to erect the 1,100 foot long center span.

The Chief Engineer of the project, Professor C. Derleth, Dean of the College of Engineering at the University of California at Berkeley, approved the plans his assistants drew up at his direction. The plan called for the construction of piers on either side of the main channel of the Sacramento River from which a cantilever frame would reach out in the direction of the other.

When ready, the distance between the two cantilevers would leave a 1,100 foot long gap to be filled in with a span to be built elsewhere and later be hoisted into place. It was built on top of a barge on the San Francisco side of the Bay.

For it to be raised and securely attached to both cantilever spans it had to be exactly the length of the gap between them. Further, for the riveters to drive the rivets in place in the pre-drilled holes, the holes could not be even a fraction of an inch out of line.

Even a considerable change of temperature with the resulting expansion or contraction at the various members could affect the fit.

All was ready for the lift and the test of the engineers' plans on the morning of May 21, 1927. A tug towed the barge and its 750 ton span and anchored it exactly under the two cantilever structures which were to receive the span resting on the barge. At times the current ran up to nine miles an hour, so the anchors had to be secure.

Prior to this, four electric sheaves had been attached to the four members to receive the 1,100 foot long span. One-and-a-half inch steel cables ran over the sheaves and had been secured to the span to be raised. The other end of each cable was secured to a large "sand box". The preloaded boxes each weighed one quarter of the 750 tons to be hoisted.

With carefully controlled power applied to each sheave, the span gradually rose. At the top of the lift, the span fitted perfectly, rivets were driven into the holes which had been drilled for them. The engineers, jubilant at the accuracy, basked in the recognition given the accomplishment their unique plan had achieved.

Bob Colin, CalTrans, Oakland

*Carquinez Bridge, lifting the center span into place, May 21, 1927.*

When a highway was paved, drivers automatically speeded up. On two-lane roads, people speeded up to pass, often without regard for curves in the highway.

So many wrecks occurred that engineers designed a center asphalt hump to divide the road into two lanes. The half-oval hump, about six inches high, was thought to keep drivers on their side of the highway. Instead, when passing, people often crossed over. When faced with an oncoming auto, they would turn their wheel abruptly, and the resulting sudden change threw the car off the edge of the pavement.

Next, engineers went with three-lane highways. That trial too was a disaster. It seemed to increase the incidents of head-on collisions.

It took a long time before engineers designed and built the system of divided highways as we know them now. It was January 27, 1947 when the first divided highway opened. This was the 12.15 miles from Vacaville to 1.3 miles north of Dixon. This was a four-lane highway divided by a wide median strip. It wasn't until July 1, 1964, that a new numbering system became effective, and the new interstate numbers and postmile signs began to appear.

Fred Emanuels photo

*Until I-80 was completed in the early 1960s, US-40 routed all truck and auto traffic through this Davis underpass and on to the city's streets.*

# San Francisco, Gateway to the Orient

In 1850, sixty-five years before men and machines hacked their way through the Central American mosquito-infested jungle to construct the Panama Canal, adventurers and gold seekers took passage from the east coast ports for Chagres, on the east coast of Panama.

For several years their only hope for reaching Panama and thus a San Francisco-bound ship, was by entrusting themselves to native boatmen first and then by walking the rest of the way to Panama City.

In the first few years following the gold find in California, only limited passage was available on the few sailing ships which stopped at Panama to replenish their stock of food and water.

Before long, the Pacific Mail Steamship Company brought large coal-burning side-wheel steamers to the Pacific Coast and established their home port in San Francisco.

The Pacific Mail had a contract with the United States Post

*While wood burning locomotives pulled trains in mid-California, coal-burning side-wheel ships carried passengers from San Francisco to Japan and China. During the Gold Rush, ships such as the Colorado on the Panama to San Francisco run, carried as many as 800 passengers per trip.*

Office to operate three vessels each month from San Francisco to Panama. The first ships, both side-wheelers, were the *S.S. California* and the *S.S. Panama.*

The *California* was 1050 tons displacement and carried 50 cabin passengers and 150 more in steerage. William H. Webb of New York was the builder. The *S.S. Panama*, 1087 tons, and the *John L. Stephens*, 1099 tons, completed the Pacific Mail original fleet.

To service the ships, Pacific Mail bought acreage in Benicia, on the Sacramento River about ten miles from San Francisco Bay. The shipping company built a machine shop, shipyard and coaling depot. About 100 men were employed there, with an average monthly payroll of $60,000.

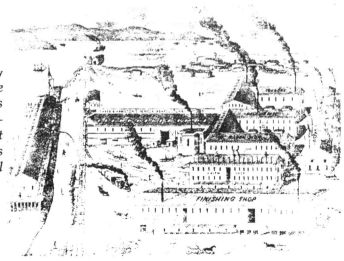

**The Jenkins Family**
*A gull's-eye vista of the great Pacific Mail docks and shops after transformation into the plant (1881) of the famous Benicia Agricultural Works.*

Whenever hauling out was called for, Pacific Mail sent its ships a few miles downstream to the U.S. Naval Shipyard at Mare Island. The navy operated a floating drydock there and welcomed commercial repairs.

All signs have since disappeared of the Pacific Mail yard in Benicia. Its location was between East 6th and East 7th Streets and ran from H Street down to the river.

(Earlier, in January 1851, the army named Benicia Arsenal the Headquarters arsenal of the Pacific Coast.)

In spite of competition, the Pacific Mail carried all the passengers that their ships could handle. In 1856, three new and larger steamers were introduced. They were *Golden Gate, Sonora,* and *Golden Age.* Unfortunately the *Golden Gate* was lost later when it burned at sea on July 25, 1862.

In 1857 Pacific Mail carried from 700 to 800 passengers to San Francisco on each trip. On the return voyage, their usual cargo included about $2 million in gold coin minted in San Francisco.

In 1865 the Pacific Mail fleet on the Panama run consisted of the *Oregon, Colorado, Sacramento, Golden City, Golden Age,* and the *Constitution.*

The Pacific Mail prospered from good management, a steady stream of immigrants to San Francisco, a good mail contract, and the largest fleet linking the Atlantic and Pacific.

When the Central Pacific Railroad cast clouds on the shipping company's good fortune by advertising that the railroad would make a coast-to-coast trip in only six days, it was more than a threat. The railroad announced a one way fare of $173 for a first class ticket. That was less than the fare from New York to Chagres, plus the one from Panama to San Francisco.

Pacific Mail turned its sights west. In 1854, Commodore Matthew Colbraith Perry had secured permission from the Japanese Government for United States commercial vessels to anchor in Yokohama harbor.

On January 1, 1867, the shipping company sent the two-year old, 318 foot long, coal-fired steamer *Montana* to Hong Kong. She had two large paddle wheels, one on each side of the wooden hull to propel her.

On March 1, 1867, Pacific Mail sent the *S.S. Herman* to Yokohama. She was only 234 feet long, short even for her time. Her side paddle wheels propelled her across the Pacific. She remained in Asia, profitably employed until 1869, when she ran aground in the Philippine Archipelago, in the Straits of Sanger. Three hundred lives were lost in the disaster.

When the *Montana* returned to San Francisco from its first trip, the company found that she had netted an $11,000 profit.

Next, Pacific Mail sent the *Great Republic* on the first trip to China. These ships led the way for what turned out to be 65 years of Pacific Mail being the principal carrier of passenger and freight traffic on the run to the Orient.

In 1879 the wholesale hardware merchants, Baker Hamilton, bought the Pacific Mail Benicia works. Thereafter, the shipping company hired outside contractors to do the necessary repair work when the ships were at the company's berths, Piers 42 and 44 on the San Francisco Embarcadero.

At approximately twenty-year intervals, Pacific Mail modernized its fleet by selling off the veterans and replacing them with ships having a larger cargo and passenger capacity.

In 1875 the Pacific Mail ships departed San Francisco for Hong Kong and Yokohama every two weeks. A branch line departed Yokohama for Shanghai, stopping at Kobe (Hiogo) and Nagasaki. The chartered ship *Str. Vasco de Gama* and the *Str. Alaska* served on this branch. The former also made voyages on the San Francisco to New Zealand run.

The new fleet in the 1880s on the Transpacific run were the steamers *City of Rio de Janiero*, *City of Peking*, *City of Sydney*, and the *City of New York*. They sailed to Honolulu and Yokohama and on to Hong Kong.

In 1904 Pacific Mail faced new competition. Japanese laborers in large numbers were filling the steerage quarters coming to California to work as stoop laborers in the fields in the San Joaquin Valley. To capture this market, the Toyo Kisen Kaisha (TKK) Steamship Company put the steamer *America Maru* on the San Francisco to Shanghai schedule.

At the same time, Pacific Mail opposed TKK with the *China*, *Mongolia*, *Siberia*, and *Korea*. The 440 foot long *China* was built in Govan, Scotland in 1889. She was driven by a single propeller powered by a triple expansion engine. Her top speed was 17

*Built in 1889 in Govan, Scotland, the S.S. China operated for many years on the Trans-Pacific service for the Pacific Mail Steamship Co. Tonnage 5060, 440 feet long, 48 foot beam. Single screw powered by a triple expansion engine. Broken up for scrap at Kowloon in 1925. Top speed 17 knots. In 1915 she carried 139 first class passengers, 41 second class, and 347 Asiatics. From author's collection.*

knots. The elapsed time San Francisco to Yokohama, with a one day stop at Honolulu, was 19 days. She had no refrigeration capacity, only an ice house measuring about 8'x8'x8' on the foredeck. In the dining salon, electric fans were non-existent, but a young, dark skinned native boy kept pulling a cord, at meal times, to keep the punka (canvas stretched over a frame hung from the ceiling) moving the trapped warm air. Pacific Mail sold the *China* in 1917 to the China Mail Steamship Company.

In 1920 Pacific Mail had 46 vessels in its fleet, most in the coastwide trade. On the Orient route it was still sending out the old *Siberia, Korea, Manchuria*, etc. When the United States Shipping Board made its new 535 foot long ships, known as 535s, available on lease, Pacific Mail contracted for five to replace the older vessels. The newer ships had accommodations for 257 first class passengers and 300 in third class. They had turbine driven power plants which delivered 12,000 shaft horsepower.

The new ships were the most efficient cargo passenger liners in the world. Yet, the government agreement gave it only a 5% return on the value of the freight shipped on their vessels.

In March 1921, Pacific Mail sent its first of the 535s on the trip to Honolulu, Yokohama, Kobe, Shanghai and Manila. Subsequently, the vessels left Pier 44 in San Francisco every other Saturday at 4 pm.

While the ships that Pacific Mail had chartered were new, the company took advantage by not servicing them as frequently as they should have. Furthermore, Pacific Mail failed to make their charter payments as soon as called for. In 1923 the Shipping Board called for bids on all their 535s. PM filed an offer on their five ships, but the Dollar Steamship Company submitted a higher bid.

Robert Dollar died on May 16, 1932, in one of the worst years of the Depression. His son, Stanley Dollar, had been running the company for several years, and his policies were unlike his father's. He was a visionary; his father was factual, knew that every dollar spent would return a dollar or more to the firm. The elder Dollar pioneered lumber sales in the Orient. The son benefited from his father's contacts there and government largesse consisting of liberal mail subsidies and loose charter agree-

*The first* President Cleveland, *one of the "535" class purchased by Robert Dollar in 1925, sporting the APL stack used after 1938. In 1924 the author sailed on her to Japan as an Ordinary Seaman at age 15.*

125

ments.

Under Stanley Dollar, money was lacking for proper maintenance. Sometimes, when ships needed to be laid up for repairs, he sent them back out. The company drew on its line of credit, established by Robert, with the Anglo-California Bank. The debt grew, and so did the charter percentage due the Shipping Board. The lines were over extended, and the combined debt had climbed to over $20 million.

The money makers, the 535s, were now 12 to 14 years old and showed a lack of maintenance. Not only had the Depression taken its toll in passenger traffic but also in freight revenues.

Until 1930 the owners had made their payments as due, but the continuing downturn in revenues caused them to ask for a moratorium on their debts.

The longshoremen's strike of 1934, which resulted in higher wages for all seafaring men on U.S. ships, nevertheless had a severe effect on the Dollar Steamship Company, causing its ships to be idle for over three months.

Another blow to the line's financial health occurred at midnight on December 11, 1937 when the *President Hoover* ran aground off the northeast coast of Taiwan. She was a total loss, though no lives were lost. But the *Hoover* represented one fourth of the firm's gross income. Most of the insurance money went to debt reduction.

When no new money could be raised to help the Dollar Company out of its financial stranglehold, J. Stanley Dollar surren-

*Upper:* The President Hoover *of the Dollar Line.*

*Lower:* APL's Presidents Cleveland *and* Wilson, *the first major liners built in the U.S. after World War II. Each was 573 feet long and carried 326 first class and 506 third class passengers. Turbine electric power. Went out of service in 1973*

dered 90% of his stock in the line to the U.S. Maritime Commission. For his part, the commission relieved Dollar of all obligations personally and retired the debt due the Anglo-California Bank.

The maritime commission thus became the new owners of the Dollar Line, and appointed William Gibbs McAdoo as president of the new corporation. At their first meeting after forming the company, the board of directors adopted the name American President Line on November 1, 1938 in San Francisco.

Just as side-wheel steamers had replaced the square riggers, so the single-screw steamships took over from the side-wheelers. Then the twin-screw luxury liners such as *President Hoover* and *President Coolidge* replaced the single propeller steamers. These deluxe passenger ships travelled a route from Manila, through Japan and Honolulu to San Francisco, and made a profit for the owners.

The next major step in travel began as a glimmer of hope in the eyes of a daydreamer who had been in a training plane during World War I. His vision was that people might travel by air between New York and San Francisco, and that he could be one of the pilots who transported people who had paid more than $100 for the privilege of riding in comfort and silence.

In 1927, Charles Lindbergh had very luckily crossed the Atlantic from New York. He had flown all the way without once being able to see straight ahead. His fuel tanks took up almost every inch of room in his cockpit. He had to sit sideways for the entire trip to Paris.

Two U.S. Army Lieutenants, L.J. Maitland and Albert F. Hegenberger, flew a tri-motor Fokker high wing monoplane from Oakland to Wheeler Field, Hawaii, in 25 hours and 20 minutes, on June 28, 1927.

James Dole, of pineapple fame, offered $35,000 for the first race contestants to fly from the mainland to Wheeler Field, Honolulu. $25,000 would go to the first place winner, and $10,000 to the owner of the second plane.

Among the contestants in the race were two who flew in the movies, who were considered by their peers among the best in the business. There were six U.S. Navy graduates from either Pensacola or Annapolis (with privately owned airships). Two others were veterans of the British Royal Air Force and the Royal Navy.

Inspectors of the Bureau of Air Commerce went over each contestant's plane before certifying it able to lift off the 7,000-foot runway in Oakland. Each was loaded with the maximum fuel it could carry.

Art Gobel, pilot, and navigator Lt. William V. Davis, U.S.N., though among the last to leave Oakland, landed at Wheeler Field in 26 hours, 17 minutes after takeoff, averaging 92 miles per hour. They received the $25,000 first prize.

Among the fourteen entrants who tried to take off were the team of Ernie Smith and Emory Bronte. They sort of made it. After flying without seeing the island of Oahu, they then sighted

Molokai, but no airfield. They made a successful landing in a tree top and collected $10,000 for their effort.

One plane took off and returned. It took off two days later and was never heard from again.

Altogether, in James Dole's race, six men and one woman, Mildred Doran, in three planes, vanished over the Pacific Ocean.

Eight years later, in 1935, Amelia Earhart made the first trans-pacific solo crossing from Honolulu to Oakland in the best time yet, 18 hours and 15 minutes, in a Lockheed Vega.

Meanwhile, twenty years after World War I, American President Lines still took travelers to the Orient. The two big luxuri-

Photo by W.T. Larkins

*Pan American's Sikorsky S-428 delivered to Alameda on January 7, 1937. Lost at sea on the way to Pago Pago, Samoa, on January 11, 1938 with Captain Musick and crew.*

130

ous vessels carried as many as 550 passengers in three classes.

Air travel across the Pacific was not affordable until after the Great Depression.

It was on October 21, 1936, when the Pan American World Airways flying boat named *China Clipper* took off from San Francisco for its destination in Manila.

Thus the long awaited smooth, silent flights were just around the corner. The lumbering flying boats were neither quiet nor comfortable.

Nevertheless, in 1937, Pan American Airways Clippers left every Wednesday at 3:00 pm for Honolulu, arriving at Pearl Harbor at 8:30 the next morning.

On the next leg of the flight, the Clipper left Honolulu at 6:30 Friday morning for Midway Island, where it put down at 3:00 in the afternoon.

The following morning it departed at 6:00 am, and crossing the International Date Line, reached Wake Island at 3:00 pm Sunday. On Monday it flew to Guam.

The next day's hop departed at 6:00 am and reached Manila eleven hours later. Passengers arrived in Hong Kong 6 hours and 35 minutes after taking off from Manila.

Pan Am charged $360 for a one way ticket to Honolulu, and $950 to Hong Kong

During World War II, the Matson Navigation Company had a contract with the United States Navy, wherein the 700 employees of its Transport Division supplied backup ground service for Navy aircraft.

At the war's end, surplus Douglas DC-4s operated by the military became surplus property and were bought up by numerous groups who had hopes of founding new airlines.

Matson bought one DC-4 and converted it as did others hoping to establish passenger service.

The airplane that Matson converted for its use, the *Sky Matson*, provided luxurious seating and dining service at tables with linen cloths and with stewardesses wearing tailored uniforms on the 12-hour flight.

Matson's initial trip left San Francisco on July 5, 1946. Passengers had the option, at no extra charge, of returning to the mainland by way of one of Matson's luxurious liners, the *Lurline* or the *Malola*, or on any of its other vessels.

Matson enjoyed an almost immediate success without any advertising expense. The privilege to advertise was denied by the Civil Aeronautics Board because the Matson Company had not yet been granted a license to fly a scheduled service, having only applied for that purpose on September 22, 1945.

At the same time Matson was succeeding, Pan American and United Airlines were flying many empty seats. Pan Am protested to the Civil Aeronautics Board that Matson was carrying passengers in spite of no federal license to do so. The result was that Matson's request for a charter was denied on July 30, 1948. Matson went out of business, selling the assets of its Air Transport Division, which later helped to found Hawaiian Airlines.

San Francisco, Gateway to the Orient

Douglas DC-4s were not the only planes flown by unscheduled and charter carriers to Hawaii and other outposts. Lockheed Constellations, and other 4-engine planes, flew under such names as Transpacific, World Airways, California Eastern, Willis Air Service, Transcontinental Air Express and Transocean Airlines.

Fifteen years after the close of World War II, on September 5, 1959, Pan American Airways set a new standard for flights across the Pacific. That day they flew the first jet powered plane, a Boeing 707, from San Francisco to Hawaii. Since then, 747s and 767s have followed. What will be the next carpet to fly on from San Francisco Gateway to the Orient?

**Photo by W.T. Larkins**
*A new Douglas DC-3 delivered to United Air Lines on February 13, 1940.*

*Pan American World Airways began Trans-Pacific service with this Boeing 707 in May 1960.*

**Photo by W.T. Larkins**

# Port of Stockton

Stockton, a link in the route to the southern mines from San Francisco, once received hoards of gold seekers travelling up the San Joaquin River to try their luck in the creek beds from Angels Camp to Columbia and Mariposa.

A half dozen steam ferries ran daily to and from San Francisco, and scores of sailing craft made the one-way trip, their owners deserting them at Stockton. Pack trains and ox-drawn wagons brought in the goods ordered from San Francisco to supply the mining camps.

The Central Valley, about 450 miles long and from 35 to 45 miles wide, grew tons of grain while Europe and the world clamored for its wheat. The least costly way to ship grain abroad was certainly by deep draft freighters, but in the early days the channel out of Stockton was littered with derelict ships and was made shallow by mine tailings washed down from the headwaters by the frequent winter rains.

In the early days when dikes formed islands of the shallow delta, the loose peat soil, dredged when building the dikes, collapsed because of the wave wash from passing vessels. Also, high water, particularly in stormy weather, sent peat back into the river.

In 1866 one out of every seven acres in Stanislaus County grew wheat. Ten years later one-fifth of the county was growing wheat.

Most of the harvest was sent down to Port Costa, Martinez, or San Francisco on riverboats or by rail where the grain was then loaded on a vessel which would deliver the grain to Europe. The cost of loading and unloading took a big bite out of the dollars returned to the growers.

By the late 1860s the valley growers were clamoring for the state to clear the Stockton channel and to dredge an outlet deep enough for ocean going vessels to come all the way up to Stockton.

Twenty-one incorporators formed the Stockton Ship Canal Company in May 1870. However, their scheme collapsed when no other investors put up any money. The company dissolved.

The Stockton Daily Independent on November 26, 1870 ran an editorial which said in part:

"If we desire to reap the advantages consequent on being the outlet and inlet of this magnificent and productive valley, and control the commerce of its predestined wealth and population, we must without delay inaugurate and push forward the one great enterprise which will, it is conceded by all, insure that result – we must build that ship canal."

As late as 1909 floods filled the river channels with soil and debris raising the stream bed and reducing its depth.

In 1908 Stockton was at the center of an 80-mile radius of one half of the state's population. Furthermore, production of wheat grown in Utah and Colorado could easily be shipped abroad from Stockton – if large freighters could lie across the docks from the trains which would bring the grain west.

In 1910 the United States Congress approved the San Joaquin Ship Channel project as recommended by the War Department. It called for dredging a nine foot deep channel, 200 feet wide, although everyone in Stockton knew that nine feet was only deep enough for stern wheel river boats.

Nine years slipped by before any significant action took place. In March 1919, following the end of World War I, Major Rand, District Engineer for the U.S. Board of Engineers for Rivers and Harbors, recommended a channel 24 feet deep. However as late as 1925 that board declined to approve Major Rand's recommendation.

In 1925 Stockton voters approved raising $3 million via a bond issue to further the effort for deep water development. Stockton Chamber of Commerce representatives went back to Washington to lobby the Committee on Rivers and Harbors in person. They pressured the members with endorsements and petitions from every organization with any clout.

In 1925 the State approved a $3 million bond issue for deep water development.

The struggle for a deep water channel all the way to Stockton was finally won when the measure was included in the Rivers and Harbor Bill of 1927. President Calvin Coolidge signed it into law on January 21, 1927.

Nevertheless, dredging didn't start until mid-1930. Ultimately a 41-mile channel was dredged to a depth of 26 feet between Stockton and Suisun Bay.

The first deep draft vessel steamed up the river in February 1933. The channel depth has since been increased to 36 feet.

Original design gave the port 1,440 linear feet of wharfage so that three oceangoing vessels could be tied up simultaneously. Subsequent construction has lengthened birth space so that ten ships can be handled at the same time. A publicly owned six and one-half mile railroad, jointly operated by the Southern Pacific, Union Pacific and Santa Fe Railroads gives equal access to the three operators.

The port operates a cotton press and grain loading equipment. The port provides storage areas for ore, lumber, cement, beans and molasses. Cotton is produced in large quantities in the San Joaquin Valley and is the single most valuable crop in the state. The Stockton waterfront compress is the only one of its type in California. It reduces the bulk of a bale to one-third of its original size. The grain terminal has the largest storage structure on the Pacific Coast, 4 1/2 million bushels.

*(continues on page 142)*

Courtesy William J. Duffy

*Upper: in the early days of California statehood, river transport was of great importance. The absence of paved roads and railways in many parts of the State left water transportation for both freight and passengers, on boats such as the above, the best way to go in the early 1900s.*

Clark Collection, Courtesy Peabody Museum

*Lower: A congregation of river steamboats at Stockton about 1920. Twelve steamboats are visible on the left side of the Stockton Channel at the yard of the California Transportation Co. The boats are well kept up and obviously in only temporary layup. At this time the river steamers played an important part in California transportation.*

*Upper: A Danish freighter at Stockton to load grain at California's largest elevator. Two mechanized towers load a combined 900 short tons per hour.*

*Lower: In Stockton's turning basin two tugs turn the ship around.*

*Upper: In order to build a ship channel as straight as possible, the dredger is cutting through Tinsley Island, (foreground) Fern, Tule Islands.*

*Lower: A freighter going downstream appears to be travelling on farm land.*

Ore and coal ships are loaded, in part, by a 1,000 foot long conveyor system which can load a ship in one day, from rail cars and the storage area.

The Port has a bulk liquid facility which in addition to petroleum, loads bulk wine, liquid fertilizer and sugar beet molasses. The Santa Cruz Cement Company has a pneumatic pipe connection to the docks from their storage silos. Lumber has been stored and shipped out from the very beginning of the Port's operation.

The longest ship to visit Stockton was the 747 foot *Madonna Lilly*, although a 900 foot long vessel can be accommodated. The largest ship in tonnage to come up channel is the 65,862 DWT *Myrine*.

In 1992 seventy-four oceangoing vessels docked at Stockton along with 58 barges.

Ships from Japan are seen at Stockton docks frequently and others have come from as far away as Greece and Turkey.

*The Port of Stockton, c.1960. California's first inland port opened in 1933 as a result of tremendous financial support from Stockton residents as well as from state and federal sources. The project involved dredging a 26-foot deep, 100-foot wide waterway through islands and existing channels in the Delta to Suisun Bay. All new port facilities were built at the confluence of the Stockton Channel with the San Joaquin River. One hundred sixty-six oceangoing vessels arrived at the facility during the first year, and the operation was so successful that the channel was deepened to 32 feet.*

*Riverboats at the San Francisco docks*

*A dredger is deepening the approach to the Stockton docks in the 1960s*

# Bridges

In 1916 James Wilkins, editor of the San Francisco Call-Bulletin began a campaign for a Golden Gate Bridge. Consequently, the City Engineer of San Francisco, Michael M. O'Shaughnessy, invited bids from interested parties. On June 28, 1921, Joseph B. Strauss, an experienced bridge builder, offered his estimate, with plans, of $27 million to build the bridge, and was subsequently offered the contract.

It took seven years to start action. Then, on December 12, 1928, the counties of Marin, Sonoma, Mendocino, Napa, San Francisco and Del Norte incorporated under the name of Golden Gate Bridge, Highway and Transportation District.

The next step was to create the funding, which took two more years. Then the voters in the counties involved approved the District, selling a $35 million bond issue.

Actual construction didn't start for another 25 months, on January 5, 1933, and was opened for vehicular traffic on May 28, 1937.

Almost 38 years later, the District began an innovation, collecting tolls in only one direction, on October 19, 1968. This was the world's first such method and has since been copied in many places. On the Golden Gate span, at first, 50 cents was the charge to southbound travelers, while the northbound motorists crossed for free.

Approximately 41 years after selling the bridge bonds, the District paid off the last of the issue. During the life of the bonds, the District paid $39 million in interest.

| | |
|---|---|
| Total length of bridge, including approaches: | 1.7 miles; 8,981 feet |
| Length of entire suspended structure without approaches: | 6,450 feet |
| Length of main span portion of suspended structure: | 4,200 feet |
| Width of bridge: | 90 feet |
| Width of sidewalk: | 10.5 feet |
| Clearance above mean high water: | 220 feet |
| Deepest foundation below mean low water: | 110 feet |
| Height of tower above deck: | 500 feet |
| Main cable diameter: | 36 3/8 inches |
| Length of one cable: | 7,650 feet |
| Number of wires on each cable: | 27,572 |

Golden Gate Bridge Highway and Transportation District

*The Golden Gate Bridge from the south and the 1855 Fort Point built so that in time of war, it could keep enemy shipping from entering San Francisco Bay. Robert David photo.*

**Golden Gate Bridge Highway and Transportation District**

*Two hundred eighty-one coaches carry more than nine million passengers each year on the Golden Gate Bridge and Transportation District service area. Robert David print.*

*Golden Gate Ferry. Ferries such as this one carried 1,466,055 passengers between Lark-spur/Sausalito and San Francisco in the year mid-1992 to mid-1993. Robert David photo.*

In 1926 the California Legislature created the Toll Bridge Authority and charged it with the responsibility for bridging San Francisco Bay to Alameda County.

The extraordinary depth of the water and the underlining land conditions required totally new techniques for placing bridge foundations. After many hours of studying the problem, engineers decided the best solution was to build two bridges, end to end on the San Francisco to Yerba Buena Island crossing.

The California State Highway Engineer, Charles H. Purcell decided to build an island between San Francisco and Yerba Buena, and connect the two spans at the Island. Construction began during July 1933. The bridge was completed in three years, six months ahead of schedule.

The greatest depth of water under the west crossing was adjacent to Yerba Buena Island, in 105 feet of water, and down 170 feet more to bed rock.

With the towers erected the wire spinning began. Riders on the ferryboats watched the spinning wheels lay individual strands from end to end, looping over the saddles at each end. When completed, the cables appeared to be one big length of wire rope. In truth, it was a series of strands, laid one on top of the other, the whole being 28 3/4 inches in diameter. The 519 foot Bay Bridge Tower, its tallest, dwarfs the Brooklyn Bridge Tower which is only 272 feet tall.

The bridge opened for vehicular traffic on November 12, 1936.

As originally built, the upper deck carried automobile traffic only, going in both directions. The lower deck carried trucks bound in either direction as well as two sets of railroad tracks used by Interurban Electric Lines.

So many head-on collisions took place on both levels, and the electric trains were taking up more room than their riders justified, that a rebuilding program to solve both concerns was initiated in 1962 and completed in October 1964. Much strengthening of the base of the roadway was done so that the upper deck could handle loaded trucks (not in the original plans) and automobiles both going westbound. The lower deck would handle the same vehicles on an eastbound course.

There was one problem to solve before this plan could work. The tunnel on Yerba Buena Island was designed for automobiles which didn't give adequate clearance for trucks (13'6"). This meant that the roadway must be lowered, which it was. During this project delays ensued because of rerouting of some traffic.

When clearance for trucks was accomplished on both east and west bound decks, one-way traffic on each level began. Traffic flowed freely and the number of accidents dropped dramatically.

The "A" line, one of five, ran from San Leandro, 105th Avenue, by way of East 14th Street through downtown Oakland to the Bay Bridge and terminated its run at the East Bay Terminal at First and Mission Streets, San Francisco. At first, all passenger cars travelled on the upper deck, while trucks in three lanes and a pair of train tracks shared the lower deck

*Taken from Yerba Buena Island after electric lights were installed*

Bob Colin photo, CalTrans Oakland

*All the ferries have disappeared from San Francisco Bay now that both the bridges are open to vehicular traffic. Approximately 350,000 autos, trucks and buses add pollutants to what was once a windswept, unsoiled atmosphere. This picture was obviously taken in 1939. The 1939-40 Golden Gate International Exposition buildings stand on Treasure Island.*

# Central Valley Project

Interest in the water problem in the state, flooding in winter and drought in summer, began in 1850 when the first California Legislature, meeting in San Jose, passed a measure requiring its staff to investigate the problem. Could they improve drainage? Could they report back how irrigation water could be saved in the rainy season? Could they devise a plan to deliver water during the rest of the year to farmers for their irrigation needs?

Little did the legislators know that their investigations would eventually result in the delivery of hydroelectric power to future cities, providing electric lights and stoves. It would also propel trains and street cars.

Eighty-one years after that first act, in 1933, the legislators approved the California State Water Plan which included the plans for constructing both Shasta Dam and Friant Dam, with a hydroelectric generating plant for each.

With an estimated cost of $170 million for the Central Valley

*Mount Shasta, Shasta Lake a few miles north of Redding. The dam is 602 feet high and 3,460 feet long.*

Project, efforts began to include the Federal Government in its cost. The initial success came in 1936 with a Federal appropriation of $12 million toward building Shasta Dam.

In April 1936 President Franklin Delano Roosevelt made an additional $15 million available and two years later added another $12.5 million.

Plans for Shasta were finalized in January 1937 for a dam 500 feet high and a hydroelectric plant which would produce 350,000 kilowatt hours. Final approval to construct came in 1938.

The U.S. Bureau of Reclamation started work on the Shasta Dam and Power Plant in September 1938, and of the Friant project in November 1939.

The $546,353,000 cost was paid 55% by the State of California and 45% by the United States.

In the winter season when an excess of water runs down the Sacramento River into the Delta, the surplus is conveyed to the San Luis Reservoir, where it is later released for irrigation. The Delta-Mendota Canal carries it from the Tracy Pumping Station, powered by Shasta Dam's Generating Plant to the San Luis Forebay where it is lifted, at a maximum rate of 4,600 second acre feet of water, 200 feet up into the San Luis Reservoir. Electric energy for the pumps comes again from Shasta but is augmented by power created when water is released into the California Aqueduct at the San Luis Generating Plant.

Normally there is salt water intrusion into the Delta water in dry seasons. At those times water released from Shasta is in-

This canal is part of the Ayhware South Unit. Approximately 60 miles long serves industrial, municipal, and

J.C. Dahilig, Bureau of Reclamation

*The Coalinga Canal supplies fresh water to the city which for the first time in its history will not have to rely on fresh water brought in by railroad tank cars, trucks or demineralized in municipal plants.*

creased to hold back this intrusion.

Bureau of Reclamation estimates hold that the cost of the San Luis Dam and Power Plant will be repaid to the United States from the sale of water and power within 50 years of its construction.

Additional dams have been built to hold back waters in small streams which would ordinarily flow into the Sacramento and San Joaquin Rivers.

The California Aqueduct delivers water over the Tehachapi Mountains to the Los Angeles Metropolitan Water District. It also sends water through tunnels in the Coast Range to communities in Monterey and Santa Cruz Counties.

There are dozens of dams astride rivers not as big as the Sacramento. In mid-California some of the larger reservoirs which hold back winter run-off of the Sierra snow pack are Folsom Lake on the American River, Lake Oroville on the Feather River, Lake Berryessa on Putah Creek, Salt Springs Reservoir, Pardee Reservoir and Commanche on the Mokolomne, Lake Pillsbury, Lake Sonoma on the Russian River. Others are Turlock Lake, Modesto Reservoir, Millerton Lake and Pine Flat Reservoir. These and many more help make it possible for the state's 31 million residents to enjoy fresh water even in years of drought.

J.C. Dahilig, Bureau of Reclamation

*This 152 mile long canal terminated about 4 miles west of Bakersfield. It takes water from Millerton Lake and supplies Fresno, Tulare, and Kern Counties.*

*This 117 mile long Delta-Mendota Canal looks north a few miles west of Patterson. It supplies irrigation water along*

J.C. Dahilig photo, Bureau of Reclamation, Water & Power Resource Service

*The San Luis Pump-Generator Plant near Los Banos. It will make available each year over a million acre-feet of new water for irrigation and 45,000 acre-feet for urban and industrial use.*

J.C. Dahilig photo, Bureau of Reclamation, Water & Power Resource Service

*Nine miles downstream from Shasta Dam, Keswick Dam and Powerplant use Shasta's water flow*

# Port Chicago

At a point along the south shore of the Sacramento River, approximately midway between Martinez and Pittsburg, on the evening of July 17, 1944, two U.S. Navy ammunition ships lay moored to the one dock of the Concord Naval Weapons Station.

The *S.S. Bryant* and the *S.S. Quinalt Victory* were receiving ammunition to be delivered to our fighting forces engaged in the Far East. Approximately 500 black sailors did the loading under the eyes of their white officers.

At exactly 10:18 pm in a flash that some observers said shot 1,000 feet in the air, both ships blew up. Three hundred twenty three people died in the explosion. More than 300 were African Americans.

Large pieces of ship superstructure and hull plates blocked the roads leading to the pier as emergency vehicles began arriving.

Amid wailing sirens, throngs of hysterical, bleeding and

*The town of Port Chicago has been erased from the picture. Two Navy transports and the pier they were tied to disappeared in a flash on the night of July 18, 1944.*

screaming men ran aimlessly about. Some dazed sailors just sat, not fully understanding the calamity that they had survived.

The two water tanks which served Port Chicago lay in a tangled wreck of pipes and bent sheet metal. Water made mud of some streets. Windows were blown out or cracked in homes and store fronts ten miles away. Even across the Oakland hills in San Leandro, windows blew out. Residents 50 miles away in western Marin County heard the sound and felt the shock of the blast.

A navy fire boat, tied up to the end of the loading pier, sank.

Strange things sometimes occur in such a calamity. In spite of damage suffered by buildings many miles away, nearby, an 18 month-old infant boy slept in his crib as a fifty pound piece of a ship's hull plate tore a hole through the roof of a home next door and ricocheted through his wall, cutting the legs off his little bed. When the parents, cut and bleeding, found their son, he was still sleeping on his mattress which by now was resting on the floor.

While three miles away a lookout on a tanker going downstream was blown off his ship into Suisun Bay, also three miles away in Montezuma Slough, occupants sleeping on the deck of their pleasure boats in the warm summer evening, neither heard the explosion nor felt the concussion. Their boats were anchored at low water below the tops of the banks of the inlet.

Miraculously, the town's theater, with a "good house" in attendance, only a half mile from the blast, survived. The walls did not collapse, and only two patrons were injured. Paradoxically, steel box cars on a nearby siding, sunken in a concrete right-of-way were crushed together like cardboard toys.

The 258 surviving black sailors were sent to the Mare Island Navy Yard to continue loading ammunition. Fifty of them refused the order to begin loading and spent the next sixteen months in a navy prison. Subsequently all fifty received sentences of 8 to 15 years confinement.

The U.S. Government paid $3,000 to each family which lost a member.

Two years after the calamity, President Harry S. Truman ordered all the military services desegregated.

Concord Historical Society

*The stern section of the* Quinault Victory *is in left center. The piling of a new pier is at water's edge. The* S.S. Bryant *which was tied to the dock has completely disappeared*

*Upper: Though protected by the concrete reventment the explosion made scrap iron of several boxcars.*

*Lower: The front of the Port Chicago Theater apparently undamaged.*

*Upper: Although the theater front remained undamaged, the side of the building was not so fortunate. A movie was being shown at the time of the explosion but no fatalities resulted.*

**Both pictures courtesy Concord Historical Society**

*Lower: Destruction in civilian residential area patrolled by army military police.*

# Henry J. Kaiser

Though Henry J. Kaiser appeared in many roles, his first as a descendant of the typical Westerner fit him well. Large of frame, with a deep throated voice, those with whom he negotiated had a difficult time seeing him as a boy born into a lower middle class family in 1882.

He left school for good after the eighth grade but had natural talents enough to become successful. He was outgoing, popular and confident.

Those characteristics didn't show when he came west from Florida to Spokane in 1906. Later he would tell the story of how he called on one hundred businesses before he found a job.

After working first for a hardware merchant, Kaiser went to work for a road paving contractor. He lost this job in 1914 through no fault of his own, but he had gained some valuable experience in seeing contracts fulfilled successfully. What did show during this job was his boundless energy, confidence and optimism.

Without any hesitation the young man started in business for himself in Vancouver, British Columbia. That city was improving its streets and Kaiser did his share of the paving.

Kaiser came to Oakland, California in 1921. His first job, other than road building, was constructing the Philbrook Dam in Butte County. He had never built a dam before, but he found men who had. This ability to pick out good men and instill enthusiasm in them was probably the most important ingredient in his make-up.

A turning point came in 1923 when the Kaiser Paving Company won a contract to build ten miles of highway. He needed gravel and lots of it for the job, but instead of buying it he opened his own pit. This source of sand and rock was at Radum, between Pleasanton and Livermore, right on the route he was building. Between 1923 and 1931, that gravel pit made him a profit of $1,375,000.

In the course of business Kaiser met the founder of the Northern California Chapter of the Associated General Contractors Association, Warren Bechtel. Bechtel advised the young man and shared many construction agreements over the years with Kaiser.

An important job came along in 1927. He accepted the subcontract to build a 750-mile road in Cuba. Under conditions which his superintendents had never seen before, his 2,000 Cuban workers, temperamental at times, chopped their way through miles of jungle and mango swamp. However, they did overcome malaria, dysentery, and pests and completed the job. Kaiser made a profit of $2.1 million on that subcontract.

As welcome as the money was, more importantly the job, its size and the fact he completed it on time, projected the man and his company over the threshold into the world of big time contractors.

With his friend Bechtel, Kaiser joined the Six Companies, a consortium organized to build the Hoover Dam on the Colorado River and later the Grand Coulee Dam on the Columbia River. Kaiser Paving and W.A. Bechtel assumed the largest share of the jobs, 30% of the contract to build the dams.

In 1938 the Grand Coulee Dam was begun and completed in 1942. Kaiser tried something new. He organized two crews to compete with each other to see who could turn out the most work. It was successful.

In 1939 a group of West Coast cement producers expected to be the successful bidders on the cement required for building Shasta Dam. Henry Kaiser had his eyes set on the same contract. His bid won by setting his price 22 cents per barrel of cement under the combine.

Unfortunately he didn't have a cement plant. However he had his engineers look for a large limestone deposit in anticipation of winning the award. They located one along Permanente Creek in Santa Clara County.

On Christmas Day in 1939 the new cement plant, Permanente

Cement in Santa Clara County, turned out its first bag of cement. With four kilns working, plant production for the first year averaged 16,000 barrels a day.

In six months Kaiser witnessed trainloads of his cement moving out of San Jose north to the Shasta Dam site.

The job also required sand and gravel. Kaiser found a quarry site only ten miles from the job. However, the local railroad men quoted him a price he considered much too high. So he had his engineers set up a ten-mile long conveyor belt from his quarry right to the dam site. On this system he delivered a thousand tons of rock and sand every hour and ran it day and night for four years, at a cost one-third less than the price the railroad had quoted him.

In late 1939, with war raging in Europe, Kaiser and his partners in the Six Companies joined the Seattle-Tacoma Shipbuilding Company, on a 50/50 basis and won the $9 million contract to build four cargo ships for the U.S. Maritime Commission.

In 1940, British ship owners came to the U.S. to find yards which could turn out, quickly, the vessels to replace those lost to the German submarines and the Luftwaffe. The British offered to pay $160,000 over the cost for sixty ships.

Kaiser's enthusiasm grew. He had never built a ship on his own. Nevertheless, he and his friends signed a contract before they even had a shipyard. That mere detail didn't faze Kaiser even a whit.

Kaiser sent his son Edgar to Portland to buy land for the

project. Edgar bought two sites, one on Swan Island and the other in Vancouver, Washington, and built his two shipyards on them.

Edgar, sensing the need to keep his workers healthy, called up Dr. Sidney R. Garfield from Oakland. Garfield, who in 1938 had established a health plan for the workers at Grand Coulee, now did the same for the Kaiser employees at Edgar's two yards. Garfield would later do the same for the employees in Richmond. He designed a 175-bed hospital in which 60 doctors tended the medical needs of the shipyard workers there. All the employees contributed 50 cents per week via payroll deduction to the Kaiser Permanente Health Plan.

Feverish work schedules, 24 hours a day, planned by competent foremen, allowed Henry Kaiser to lay the keel for the *Ocean Vanguard* on April 14, 1941, almost eight months before the attack on Pearl Harbor. That ship was the first of 747 vessels to slide down the ways from the Kaiser yards into San Francisco Bay in Richmond.

Pearl Harbor focused the worker's attention on the job before them like no other event could.

By the end of 1942, 80,000 men and women were working at the four Kaiser shipyards in Richmond and Portland.

Henry J. Kaiser moved more people to the West Coast than any man had ever moved people anywhere.

While the Richmond yards finished up by building 747 ships, the Portland yards turned out 743. No other contractor has ever surpassed Kaiser's performance of building 1,490 ships in such a short time.

Further, no other health plan can say it cares for as many as Kaiser's. In 1994 over two million members were enrolled. At the same time, more than six million have been cared for since the founding of the plan.

This phenomenal achievement is the result, in part, by Kaiser Permanent accepting individuals to membership, after accepting only groups initially.

Kaiser Industries

*Overhead view of the Richmond shipyards, about 1943*

# Bay Area Rapid Transit System (BART)

The Bay Area Rapid Transit System was the largest single public works project ever undertaken in the United States by the local citizenry.

The concept of such a system, utilizing an underwater bay tube connecting San Francisco and the East Bay, was not new. The builder of the Panama Canal (1915), Major General George T. Goethals, in 1920 made public his proposal for building such a tube in order to solve the acute transportation problems facing the two communities.

In 1951 the State Legislature created a 26-man San Francisco Bay Area Rapid Transit Commission composed of representatives from each of the nine counties which touch the bay.

Acting on the commission's recommendations, the legislature in 1957 formed the San Francisco Bay Area Rapid Transit District comprising the five counties of Alameda, Contra Costa, Marin, San Francisco and San Mateo.

Between 1957 and 1962, engineering plans were developed for a system that would usher in a new era in rapid transit. Electric trains would run on grade-separated rights-of-way, reaching maximum speeds of 75-80 miles per hour, averaging 45 mph, including station stops.

By midsummer 1961, the final plan was submitted to the supervisors of the five counties for approval. San Mateo County Supervisors were cool to the plan. Citing the high costs when adequate service existed from Southern Pacific commuter trains, they voted to withdraw from the district in December 1961.

Marin County also withdrew, pointing to their marginal tax base as too small to absorb the proposed cost.

Subsequently, in 1965 the enabling legislation was changed to apportion the BART Board with three Directors from each of the remaining three counties.

The new plan revised to a three county District required a 60% vote of the electorate. It passed with 61.2% approval. The voters endorsed a $792 million bond issue to finance a 71.5-mile high speed system consisting of 33 stations serving 17 communities in the three counties. However, in 1962 the total cost of the system was projected upward to $996 million.

BART construction began on June 19, 1964 with President Lyndon Johnson presiding over ground breaking ceremonies for the 4.4-mile Diablo Test Track between Concord and Walnut Creek.

The 3.2-mile bore through the Berkeley-Oakland hills was

completed in February, 1967.

The BART Transbay Tube, stretching 3.6 miles on the floor of the Bay, at its maximum depth of 135 feet below the surface, is both the longest and the deepest vehicular tube in the world, or was until the completion of the tube connecting France and England in 1994.

The huge construction effort reached its peak in 1969 when the construction force of 5,000 worked on the San Francisco subway and other parts of the system, and the weekly payroll was over $1 million.

Despite the complex problems of forming a subway tube through loose sand, the BART project was completed with one of the best safety records in heavy construction.

The job was completed in August, 1969. Construction is highlighted by the 57 sections laying on the bottom of the Bay. It took six years to complete hooking them together.

In August, 1970 the first test prototype car was delivered. By early 1971 ten test prototype cars ran on the Fremont line in round-the-clock tests.

The first part of the system to open was the 28 miles between MacArthur and Fremont stations. The first day of revenue service was Monday, September 11, 1972 on that same line. Service to San Francisco began on September 16, 1974.

According to BART literature, the system now carries 250,000 one-way passengers daily, reducing the number of cars on the road by approximately 175,000.

As of 1995, no passenger has ever met an accidental death on BART, a record unequaled by any other transit system in the United States.

After two decades of serving more than a billion riders, BART is building extensions to its system. Extending the Concord line envisions stretching that terminal to Antioch, an eight-mile addition, servicing two new stations. In Alameda County new tracks will connect Hayward with Pleasanton, fourteen miles away. Across the Bay, a line from the Daly City station is under construction to Colma, 1.6 miles long. BART Directors are studying the feasibility of 6.4 new miles of additional track to the San Francisco Airport. Preliminary studies include a 5.4 stretch of new track from Fremont, through Irvington, to Warm Springs. Current plans, in 1995, call for this line to be in operation in 1999.

**Bay Area Rapid Transit District**

*Since beginning service in 1973 BART has never had*
*a passenger fatality*

# Port of Sacramento

In 1947 the voters of Sacramento and Eastern Yolo Counties approved the formation of the Sacramento-Yolo Port District, and approved a $3.75 million bond issue for paying some of the construction costs. Their purpose was at least two fold.

The port would make it possible for oceangoing vessels to load in Sacramento, keeping the revenue from it in Sacramento, rather than sending it to San Francisco.

Secondly, they saw an opportunity to store agricultural products, which came in less than large enough quantities for shipping, until loads could be combined into one shipment. Growers then might benefit from the lower freight weights then available.

However, the Sacramento River as nature made it consisted of many sharp courses. The turns wouldn't allow a large ship to proceed.

The port must have a nearly straight channel down to deep

*(continues on page 184)*

**Port of Sacramento**

*The port one month before opening in 1963*

*The first vessel to come up the 42-mile long channel to Sacramento arrived in July 1963.  The* Taipei Victory *loaded rice and pine logs for Japan.*

water. Hence, between 1955 and 1962 large earth moving trac-
tor-scrapers and drag lines scooped a 42-mile ditch, 30 feet deep,
out of what had been Sacramento County farm land. A hydraulic dredge helped in the process. The ditch has no perceptible
turns in it.

From the port the ditch ends a short distance above Rio Vista,
where deep water is available

The federal government aided the port by assuming part of
the cost of digging the ditch.

**Port of Sacramento**
*An empty ship going to load at Sacramento*

*A tug has helped turn around a loaded ship, 1971.*

By 1962 the port had built enough piers and wharves to berth five ships at one time. They also had 80,000 square feet of covered and paved storage plus additional uncovered area.

The first ship to come up the canal, the *Taipei Victory,* loaded 5,050 tons of rice for Okinawa and 25,000 board feet of pine logs for Japan.

The port built a thriving market for wood chips for paper and cardboard manufacture. A mountain of wood chips could be seen by motorists on the nearby Interstate-80. Japanese wood chip vessels were loaded by the port conveyor system.

The *MV Ambia Fair,* a 790-foot long vessel is the longest ship to come up the ship channel to Sacramento. She arrived in 1981.

In 1983, at the twentieth anniversary of the port, the announcement was made that 2,600 vessels had entered the port bearing the flags of 41 nations.

The depth of the ship canal at 30 feet is too shallow to attract some of the largest vessels now in use. The port officials have been trying to attract enough funding to deepen the ditch another five feet. In 1994, eight of the 24.5 miles were deepened.

Another very steep obstacle to be overcome is the pair of natural gas pipe lines belonging to the Pacific Gas & Electric Company, which cross the Sacramento River from Collinsville to Antioch. They lie at a depth of thirty feet, another bar to the large carriers. So far, PG&E will not pay the cost of lowering the lines, and the Port cannot afford it, which would likely come to about $10 million.

In 1981, Free Trade Zone #139 opened for business. Merchandise brought into the United States to a free trade zone is not charged the usual duty. It is assessed the duty when it leaves the zone. This is an incentive for importers to anticipate future sales. The port benefits from the rent it charges the zone.

In 1992 the first New Zealand pine logs were imported. Since timber cutting restrictions have been imposed on western states since 1992, New Zealand pine logs have found a market in the United States. They are imported through the Port of Sacramento.

A 47-acre log yard is leased by Sierra Global Enterprises, a division of Bordges Timber of Shingle Springs, California. At the yard, logs cut in the Sierra are decked, scaled, sorted, and then delivered to the adjacent log ship berth.

Continental Grain Company in New York exports California rice through the port. It is shipped in 50-kilo bags, loaded on slings. They load at the rate of 170 tons per gang of longshore-men per hour. In the old system of loading first on pallets they used to average only about 35 tons per hour.

Cargill, one of the world's largest grain traders, has a long term lease on the port grain elevator. In addition to handling wheat, Cargill ships safflower from the port docks.

Norwegian flag ships bring fertilizer to Sacramento. Delivering it to the proximity of where it is used is economical, lowering the cost to distributors.

On more than 1,000 acres of privately owned land on the south side of the deep water channel, the port has plans to construct industrial parks as they are needed. Since 1977, Unocal has operated an anhydrous ammonia/urea fertilizer plant on the first bend in the channel.

In 1993, 83 ocean going vessels and 15 barges visited the Port of Sacramento.

The latest figures available show that from July 1993 through June 1994, tonnage handled by the port topped the previous year by 22% to 1,368,431 tons. Fiscal year 1994 revenue of $12.25 million exceeded the $10,126,127 million of fiscal 1993.

Scores of jobs are evidence of the economic benefits, and there are many more related positions filled which are out of sight, created by the Port of Sacramento.

*This vessel is loading wood chips for Japan.*

# Loma Prieta Earthquake

On October 17, 1989 at 5:04 pm, and eleven miles below the surface of the earth, the Pacific plate suddenly jolted 6.2 to the northwest and rode 4.3 feet up over the North American plate. This movement of the earth's crust came to be known as the Loma Prieta earthquake. The magnitude registered 7.1 on the Richter scale.

Loma Prieta is the name of a mountain approximately nine miles northeast of Santa Cruz and 60 miles south-southeast of San Francisco.

During the next ten seconds the earth rupture spread about 26 miles northwest and southeast and about eight miles upward, stopping about three miles below the surface.

Moments after the shock, 62 persons either died or suffered fatal injuries. In addition, 3,757 were injured. Two died in Santa Cruz when an unreinforced brick wall fell on them.

In San Francisco, 66 miles north, 44,000 people sitting in

*A section of the upper deck fell when the bridge's foundation shook on October 17, 1989. The bridge was closed for over thirty days.*

Candlestick Park awaited the beginning of the first game of the World Series. The stadium moved only slightly; there was no panic. Out near the eastern shore of San Francisco Bay, a section of the upper deck of the Bay Bridge fell onto the lower deck. A motorist missed seeing the fallen roadway, and drove into the void and died from the resulting injuries. The bridge remained unusable for one month.

The worst damage was at the Cypress Street section of the two-tiered Interstate-880. The upper deck collapsed onto the cars on the lower deck, crushing them flat and killing the occupants.

Ten miles away, in the Marina District in San Francisco, several apartment houses collapsed. One caught fire and was totally consumed. The entire neighborhood had been built on mud fill making it extremely unstable and resulting in liquifaction. The area had been part lagoon and part tidal swamp in 1915, before bay mud was pumped in for the location of the Panama-Pacific International Exposition. The area of the exposition is now the Marina District.

Structures built on a rock base generally survived the Loma Prieta Earthquake. In addition, no structure failed that was engineered to the building standards required in 1989.

San Francisco Chronicle

*An apartment building crushes a parked car in the Marina District where broken gas lines would later spark voracious fires*

San Francisco Chronicle

*Shock waves turn the hard mud base of San Francisco's Marina District into mud, tossing buildings off their foundations and into the street.*

*Tunnel view of Yosemite Valley*

**National Park Service photo**

# Yosemite Valley

People who study such things tell us that Yosemite began forming about 500 million years ago. At that time the Sierra Nevada region lay under an ancient sea. Thick layers of sediment accumulated on the sea bed and eventually were folded and twisted and ultimately were thrust above sea level.

Simultaneously molten rock welled up from deep within the earth and cooled, slowly forming granite.

About 85 million years ago, an ice age was breaking up, and water and glaciers began carving out the canyons we see today.

Yosemite is full of natural wonders, and fortunately it was given to the State of California on October 1, 1890. In effect the state was deemed a stricter guardian than the distant federal government. The danger to be protected was twofold. One lay with eager lumber companies wanting to cut down the Giant Sequoias for the long straight boards they would have to sell at premium prices. The other threat came from well financed mining interests with a passion for a virgin territory which showed traces of numerous minerals above ground.

The Yosemite Valley may be the world's best known glacier-carved granite canyon. It has sheer walls and a flat floor. In 1993 almost four million (3,983,749) visitors came to camp, hike, backpack, or just gaze at nature's handiwork.

About 6,000 hikers each year choose from 800 miles of trails. Campers select their camps from 1,841 sites in the 27 camp-grounds.

The Giant Sequoias, those mammoth trees which grow in 75 different groves at between 4,500 and 7,000 feet above sea level attract a majority of the visitors to Yosemite. John Muir, the Scot born naturalist, wrote this about the Sequoias, "The Big Tree is Nature's forest masterpiece and so far as I know, the greatest of living things."

Outstanding individual Giant Sequoias are from 2,500 to 3,000 years old. They only die when they topple over as the result of stronger winds than their roots can resist. They grow only on the western slopes of the Sierra Nevada in California.

Spectacular views abound throughout Yosemite National Park. Almost half the visitors who come to view them come from other countries. The United Kingdom, Germany and Canada are home to most of them. One of the most visited view-points is Glacier Point. This overlook is 3,000 feet above the valley floor and is home to camera clicking crowds. From here a visitor sees waterfalls on both sides of the great canyon, Half

196

Dome, that block of granite which rises to 8,842 feet, and the four-mile hiking trail down to the valley floor.

Crane Flat is both a pleasant forest and a mountain meadow.

Tuolomne Meadows , at 8,600 feet, is a large alpine meadow and a trailhead for the Muir Trail and for the climb to 13,114 foot high Mt. Lyell.  In early summer, hikers see the abundance of wildflowers and wildlife.

Winter skiing, snowshoeing, and ice skating draw many enthusiastic visitors.

The Tioga Pass Road, except in winter when it is closed by snow, rises to 9,945 feet above sea level, is a spectacular 39-mile drive.

Wawona, where Galen Clark built the first hotel in 1857 in what later became Yosemite National Park, is at the southern entrance to Yosemite.  It is also home to the nearby Mariposa Grove of the Giant Sequoias.

The uplift of granite, the glaciers and streams have built better than man could.  Nature has been kind and abundant to this National Park. In this century man has become the biggest threat to Yosemite's well being.

*The General Grant Tree in Kings Canyon National Park*

# Bibliography

Atherton, Gertrude. *The Splendid Idle Forties*. New York: The Macmillan Co., 1902.

Bancroft, H.H. *California Pioneer Register*. Register Publishing Co., 1964.

BART. *A History of BART, 1946 – 1972*. San Francisco: Bay Area Rapid Transit District.

Blaisdell, Marilyn. *San Francisciana Photographs of Three Worlds Fairs*. San Francisco: Marilyn Blaisdell, 1994.

*California Water Resources*. Department of Public Works, November 1974.

Caughy, J.W. *California Gold Rush*. Berkeley: University of California Press, 1948.

Dakin, Susanna B. *Lives of William Hartnell*. Stanford, 1949.

Davis, Winfield J. *History of California Political Conventions*. California State Library, 1890.

De Voto, Bernard. *The Year of Decision, 1846*. Little Brown, 1972.

Dillon, Richard. *Great Expectations*. Benicia Heritage Society, 1977.

Dunscumb, Guy L. *Northwestern Pacific Railroad*. Redwood City, California: Fred A. Stidt, 1964.

Dunscumb, Guy L. *A Century of Southern Pacific Steam*. Modesto, California: Dunscumb, 1963.

Duffy, William J. *Sutter Basin and Its People*. Davis, 1962.

Edward, Ron. *Airliners*. July / August, 1984.

Franks, Kent and Lamber. *Early Oil*. Texas A & M Press, 1945.

Golden Gate Bridge and Transportation District. *Highlights, Facts and Figures*. 1994.

Hardeman, Nicolas. *Heartland and Harbor*. Stockton: Holt-Atherton, 1943.

Harlan, George B. *San Francisco Bay Ferry Boats*. Howell-North, Berkeley, 1943.

Heyl, Erik. *Early American Steamers*. Buffalo, New York, 1953.

James, George W. *In and Out of the Old Missions*. Boston: Little Brown, 1924.

Kemble, John H. *San Francisco Bay Maritime History*. Cornell Press, 1957.

Lyman, George W. *John Marsh Pioneer*. New York: Scribner, 1930.

Menson, E.C. *San Francisco – Oakland Bay Bridge*. 1936.

Muir, John. *Yosemite*. New York: Century, 1912.

Nevin, John. *APL and Its Forebearers*. University of Delaware Press, 1987.

Nevins, Allan. *Fremont Pathmarker of the West*. New York: Frederick Ungar, 1955.

News Staff. *Loma Prieta Earthquake, San Francisco*. San Francisco: Chronicle Books, 1989.

Oakeshott, Gordon. *Earthquakes and Volcanos*. McGraw Hill, 1976.

Rowse, A.L. *The Earth Encompassed*. World Publishing Co., 1966.

Scott, E.B. *Saga of Lake Tahoe*. Crystal Bay: Sierra Tahoe Publishing Co., 1957.

Thomas and Witt. *San Francisco Earthquake*. New York: Stein and Day, 1971.

Thompson, Robert A. *Russian Settlement in California*.

U.S. Department of the Interior. *Loma Prieta Earthquake*. Menlo Park, 1990.

Walker, Bryce. *Earthquake*. Time Life Books, 1982.

U.S. Water Project Authority. *History of the Central Valley Project*. 1940.

White, Gerald T. *Formative Years in the Far West*. Meredith, 1962.

Wiltsee, Ernest A. *Gold Rush Steamers of the Pacific Coast*. Grabhorn, 1938.

# Index

# Index

# Index

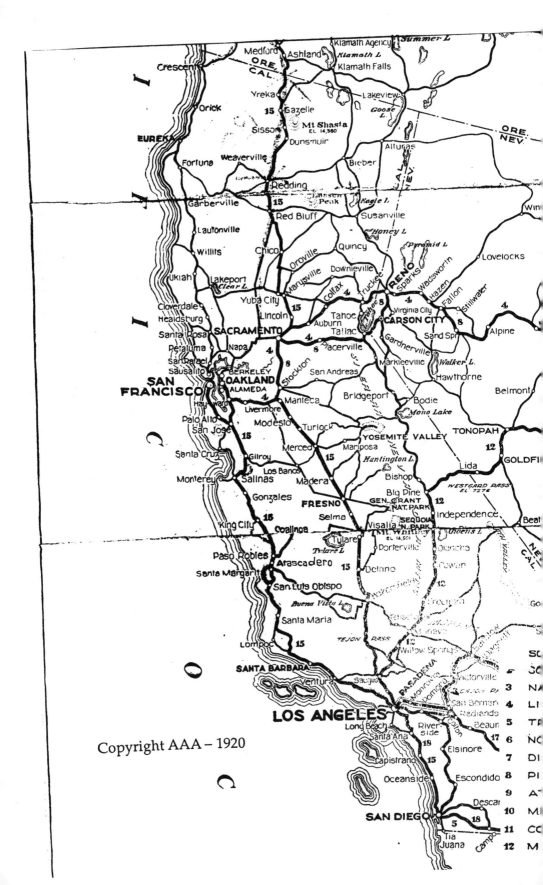

Copyright AAA – 1920